Magnolia Grace Gardens is a scripture-inspired, imaginative and creative collection of poetry. It will encourage readers to deepen their faith roots as it illuminates the power and beauty of drawing closer to the restorative and transformational desires in God's heart for each one of us.

—**Larry Law, Founder and CEO of Living Water Resorts, Collingwood Ontario.**

Magnolia Grace Gardens is a wonderful collection of inspiring poems. My encouragement would be to take your time and ponder them slowly for maximum benefit. The scripture references at the end add so much value to each one. Nancy's gift of poetry will be a blessing to you!

—**Rev Jeff Laird, Assistant to the Superintendent—Ministry, Eastern Ontario and Nunavut District, The Pentecostal Assemblies of Canada**

In *Magnolia Grace Gardens,* Nancy brings her deep love relationship with Christ into words that uplift and transcend. For just a moment you enter into this love and are blessed by a sweet Presence within her writing …

—**Lorna Tatomir, Educator, LEI Canada**

In *Magnolia Grace Gardens,* Nancy (Warwick) Kingdon captures and conveys biblical insight in beautiful poetic expression. She draws from the well of personal experience and offers the reader applications of truth that can readily be taken to heart.

—**Rev. Craig Burton, General Secretary Treasurer,**
The Pentecostal Assemblies of Canada

In *Magnolia Grace Gardens,* Nancy Kingdon has once again created a masterful collection of soul-stirring poetry gathered under ten themes, each of which provide opportunity to "park, pause and ponder" on each line, both written and not. Each poem is wonderfully crafted with an imaginative flair to express and evoke God's truth with a sense of transcendency. In these beautifully written words, you will find inspiration and resonance within your spirit. Taken in small doses, they'll bring health to your soul.

—**Dr. Don Moore, PhD, Executive Director,**
Canadian Christian Business Federation

Magnolia Grace Gardens is another uniquely creative collection of poems that will encourage and thrill your soul. Nancy has a beautiful ability to convey deep truths in an easy-to-understand, Christ-centred way. Use this book as part of your devotional reading and let it spur you on to desire more of the presence of the Lord.

—**Rev. Rick Busse, Lead Pastor,**
Evangel Pentecostal Church, Oshawa, Ontario

This newest collection of poetry from Nancy Kingdon refreshes, inspires, and instructs. Her words connect us to scripture and one another as she shares her unique perspectives on God's presence and love for us. *Magnolia Grace Gardens* is a luminous and lifting work to ponder and enjoy!

—**Dr. Melina L. Gallo, Ed.D. Director,**
Light of the World Learning, Chicago, Illinois, www.LightOfTheWorldLearning.org

Nancy Kingdon has done it again! As she did with her previous book, *Arising Rejoicing*, with *Magnolia Grace Gardens*, Nancy has written an impressive collection of inspiring poetry based on scripture. Nancy's faith shines through her words. And they are compelling words—each word chosen carefully for maximum impact. Even the arrangement of the words on the page showcases Nancy's creativity and skill.

—Rev Christopher Kennedy, Senior Pastor,
Shepherd of the Hills Lutheran Church, San Antonio, Texas

Magnolia Grace Gardens is a must read and an absolutely delightful collection of poems! I am spellbound by this wonderful and powerfully imaginative amalgamation of poems written by Nancy (Warwick) Kingdon, which bring us nearer to God and shine light on His mercy for us. These poems teach us that putting our faith in God is both rewarding and trustworthy.

—**Christina Alexander, MBA (Human Resources and Finance)**

In her newest collection of devotional poetry, *Magnolia Grace Gardens*, Nancy (Warwick) Kingdon again takes us on a powerful journey. As fragrance from garden blooms can transport us into beautiful memories and awareness, so her prayerful poetry becomes sweet, fragrant incense drawing us into the healing and restoring presence of God. There His mercy and grace abound and we are restored to our Faith Roots in the loving presence of our Lord and Saviour, Jesus Christ.

—Rev. Carey Jo Johnston, M.Div. Managing Director,
Literacy & Evangelism Canada, www.literacyevangelism.ca

Nancy (Warwick) Kingdon has crafted this collection of devotional poems as she journeys in prayer with God. The creative words are food for reflection and, yes, our own conversations with the Lord. Several felt like personal invitations to something deeper, like "The Sabbath Rest," "Building Bible College Capacity," and "Maggie's Place Beckons: Come!" Take this little gem as an invitation for you to be drawn closer to Jesus.

—**Rev. Valerie Penney, Prayer Mobilization Coordinator,
Mission Global, PAOC, Port Perry, Ontario.**

Nancy Kingdon

Magnolia Grace Gardens
A Collection of Devotional Poetry

MAGNOLIA GRACE GARDENS
Copyright © 2025 by Nancy Kingdon

All rights reserved. Neither this publication nor any part of this publication may be reproduced or transmitted in any form or by any means, electronic or mechanical, including photocopying, recording or any information storage and retrieval system, without permission in writing from the author.

Unless otherwise indicated, scripture quotations are taken from THE HOLY BIBLE, NEW INTERNATIONAL VERSION®, NIV® Copyright © 1973, 1978, 1984, 2011 by Biblica, Inc.® Used by permission. All rights reserved worldwide. • Scripture quotations marked (RSV) are taken from the Revised Standard Version of the Bible, copyright © 1946, 1952, and 1971 the Division of Christian Education of the National Council of the Churches of Christ in the United States of America. Used by permission. All rights reserved. • Scripture quotations marked (NLT) are taken from the Holy Bible, New Living Translation, copyright © 1996, 2004, 2015 by Tyndale House Foundation. Used by permission of Tyndale House Publishers, Inc., Carol Stream, Illinois 60188. All rights reserved. • Scripture quotations marked (ESV) are taken from The ESV® Bible (The Holy Bible, English Standard Version®). ESV® Text Edition: 2016. Copyright © 2001 by Crossway, a publishing ministry of Good News Publishers. The ESV® text has been reproduced in cooperation with and by permission of Good News Publishers. Unauthorized reproduction of this publication is prohibited. All rights reserved.

ISBN: 978-1-4866-2647-2
eBook ISBN: 978-1-4866-2648-9

Word Alive Press
119 De Baets Street Winnipeg, MB R2J 3R9
www.wordalivepress.ca

Cataloguing in Publication information can be obtained from Library and Archives Canada.

Magnolia Grace Gardens: A Collection of Devotional Poetry seeks to offer an imaginative faith vision for the healed and restored church that is here whimsically given the name "Magnolia Maggie." These poems seek to draw hearts closer to God's heart in worship, hope, and awe. Our life story is embedded in Jesus' story. Poetry's garden can help to create a cathedral heart space of holiness and reverence that has the potential to deepen FAITH ROOTS and confirm our place as God's chosen inheritance.

Paul's prayer for the church in Acts 20:32 is the goal of this poetry collection: *"Now I commit you to God and the word of his grace, which can build you up and give you an inheritance among all those who are sanctified."*

Note that there are ten chapters, each with fifteen poems, that spell out the FAITH ROOTS theme:
Faith, Authority, Inheritance, Transformation, Hope
Restoration, Oneness, Obedience, Trust, Strength

CHAPTER 1
Faith

TABLE OF CONTENTS

Answered Prayer	2
Caring Friends	3
Expand Belief	4
Faith Matters	5
Faith Seeds Growing	6
Faith Takes Action	7
Faith's Chair Lift	8
Giving Kindness	9
Lessons from Jabez	10
The Sabbath Rest	11
Sanctuary Space	12
Seeking God	13
Solitude: What Is It?	14
Twenty Words	15
Vision's Footsteps	16

Themes in this chapter include faith and prayer.

Answered Prayer

Lord Jesus, please pray for us and connect
us with Your strong faith, creating direct
links, uniting heaven and earth as one
desire, prayers spoken, victories won!

authority supreme, fullness flowering
confidence in Jesus' name empowering
hearts to believe, overcoming all doubt,
as in the name of Jesus we now shout!

together our prayers, like chain roots long
stretch from one heart to another, so strong
God's Presence of grace is felt in garden,
as every prayer's answered: "Yes and amen!"

Inspiration for this poem comes from the power of answered prayers. See Isaiah 37:20b–22, 29. Note that because Hezekiah prayed, God moved—defeating his enemy.

Caring Friends

For friends to lower sick man through the roof
Requires faith and trust in Jesus' power;
Their caring hearts reveal their compassion
And reflect the heart of God toward all.

Yet the fragility of the sick man,
Dependent on friends and vulnerable,
Also highlights God's compassionate grace—
To meet each one of us, where we are found.

When we carry others, or are carried,
We humble ourselves to depend on God;
Prayer builds a caring community
Connecting us with God and one another.

But no extended warranties exist
To frame wishes into reality.
Instead, we must trust God is always good,
Knowing us and wanting what's best for us.

See Mark 2:4–5.

Inspiration for this poem came from reading Kate Bowler's article "The Roof Always Caves In: How Being Human Means Living with No Extended Warranties."[1]

---

[1] Kate Bowler, "The Roof Always Caves In: How Being Human Means Living with No Extended Warranties," *Comment: Public Theology for the Common Good*, 40 (4), Fall 2022, 17–22.

Expand Belief

Holy Spirit, May You EXPAND BELIEF in Christ Jesus, as our Saviour, to:

        E   X   P   A   N   D

B   Bless belief in hearts today;   B

E   Empower trust in God's way;   E

L   Love passionately always;   L

I   Instruct wisely all our days;   I

E   Excel in knowing God's heart;   E

F   Free minds—belief to expand!   F

        E   X   P   A   N   D

"Simon Peter answered him, 'Lord, to whom shall we go? You have the words of eternal life. We have come to believe and to know that you are the Holy One of God'" (John 6:68–69).

Faith Matters

Want to avoid a fall?

*If you do not stand firm in your faith
you will not stand at all!*

What does this mean?
standing firm in faith
means

believing God's Word is trustworthy—truth's proof!
taking captive thoughts, testing them with God's Word;
choosing what is right, what is just, what pleases God!

remember …
Without faith it's impossible to please God!

"*If you do not stand firm in your faith, you will not stand at all*" (Isaiah 7:9b).

"*But the Lord will be exalted by his justice, and the holy God will be proved holy by his righteous acts*" (Isaiah 5:16).

"*And without faith it is impossible to please God, because anyone who comes to him must believe that he exists and that he rewards those who earnestly seek him*" (Hebrews 11:6).

Faith Seeds Growing

Stars   of   Wisdom
s   o   w
                                        faith's
s e e d s   fullness
                                        working
                     oneness
                            d e e d s…
                                        plentiful
                                        grass-thick
s   o   d   covering
                                        our land
with worship's wonder!
                              green grass
                                      growing grand!

Faith Takes Action

Faith always requires action—a stepping out to do something!
Expect miracles, ask for them, BELIEVE and your heart'll sing!
But more than this, you must move forward into an action plan,
Fighting every thought that denies God's best for you and your clan.
Do you have a thigh muscle that cramps, pain howling like a beast?
Believe you're healed? Step out and WALK! Demonstrate muscle released!
Is your mind cluttered with fears? Step out and do that thing you fear!
When God is with you, His authority is yours, standing near.
When you pray according to His will, He listens, hears, answers;
Is anything too hard for God, even the threat of cancers?
No! God's able and always wants for each child to pass faith's test,
So pray—TAKE ACTION—but trust God's plan to bless, doing what's best!

Faith's Chair Lift

Do you lack wisdom? Then ask God today;
Want to be fruitful? Then start now to pray!

Thank You, Lord, for giving what we so lack,
Strength to fight our enemy's strong attack!

    L   Love is ours because our God is love!
    A   Anointing given, to empower;
    C   Creativity ours, as grace's gift.
    K   Knowing God inspires discernment.

Fills us afresh with all that we need
To become fruitful, planting truth's seed!

Give us righteousness's revelation,
Ears to hear, eyes to see salvation!

Like stars we'll shine, each with unique gift
To lead many forward, faith's chair lift!

"Those who are wise will shine like the brightness of the heavens, and those who lead many to righteousness, like the stars for ever and ever" (Daniel 12:3).

Giving Kindness

Be an unsung hero today, God's way;
Ordinary people can do kind things:
As volunteers, serving communities,
As employees, encouraging colleagues.

Be an unsung hero, faithfulness's way,
Ordinary people doing kind things:
Serving as neighbourhood organizers,
Quietly caring for loved ones and friends.

Be an unsung hero, ready to pray,
Ordinary people doing kind things:
Working with commitment to help others,
Praying for someone in need of God's strength.

When God is your song, the glory is His!
Just remember to submit what you do …
Anything you give, however small 'tis
Matters to the person you give it to!

Inspiration for this poem comes from a story and quotation shared with listeners at Queen Elizabeth II's funeral on September 19, 2022: "To be inspirational, you don't have to save lives or win medals. I often draw strength from meeting ordinary people doing extraordinary things: volunteers, carers, community organisers and good neighbours; unsung heroes whose quiet dedication makes them special. They are an inspiration to those who know them."[2]
—At the Olympic Games in Rio de Janeiro, 2016

---

[2] "The 17 Most Memorable Quotes the Queen Shared throughout Her 70-Year Reign," Harper's Bazaar, accessed November 23, 2024, https://harpersbazaar.com.au/the-queens-most-memorable-and-inspirational-quotes/.

Lessons from Jabez

called "more honorable" than his brothers,
Jabez had a tough name to overcome;
since his name sounds like the Hebrew word for "pain,"
prayers he teaches we will want to retain!

"blessing's influence," he pleads; "enlarge my
territory"; he asks for God's favour,
then, "let your hand be with me!" his heart's cry;
"keep me from harm," protection held high!

since God answered his prayers, helping discern
right from wrong, calling him "honourable!"
we, too, can overcome any label,
inherited lies from youth's cruel fable.

his blessing and influence prayers answered
Jabez knows God's favour and protection;
we too can learn from Jabez how to pray
for favour's godly influence to stay!

Read: 1 Chronicles 4:9–10

Inspiration for this poem came from a sermon preached by Rev. Chris Canning on August 20, 2023 at Evangel Church, Oshawa Ontario.

The Sabbath Rest

T   Today, dear God, I make every effort to enter Your rest;
H   Help me to enter—believing, obeying, free from all doubt
E   Empowered to enter, by Your new covenant, Jesus' blood!

S   Sabbath Rest transforms our lives, refreshes, revives, and renews
A   All who step up into this promised land, this promise of peace,
B   Blood-price paid by Jesus Christ Himself, our Saviour, Redeemer,
B   Bringing hope to humanity, defeating strongholds of sin
A   As hearts repent, turning toward Jesus, our Saviour and Lord,
T   Trusting in God's gift of grace, God's solution for mankind's sin
H   Hearts hearing God's Word, obeying truth, rest by faith receiving!

R   Rest, the Sabbath rest from our works, is a promise from our God
E   Empowering us to walk not in our strength, but God's anointing,
S   Secure in our relationship of obedience to God,
T   Trusting God to teach us, carry us, strengthened, held close to Him.

"For anyone who enters God's rest also rests from their works, just as God did from his. Let us, therefore, make every effort to enter that rest, so that no one will perish by following their example of disobedience" (Hebrews 4:10–11).

CHAPTER 1: FAITH

Sanctuary Space

Entering into Your Presence, dear Lord,
I find peace, deliverance, and cleansing
From cluttered head space with jarring discord;

Today I am battling bitterness roots,
My need to be in control destructive,
Like weeds choking out prayer's perfumed shoots;

I must learn to believe what I don't see
Faith promised, with answered prayers yet to come,
Doors still closed I want opened, without key;

My most vulnerable spot is attacked,
Why? God is touching family, at last!
Soul space reaching for love, grace-impacted;

Seeking to enter sanctuary space,
Where miracles appear as joyful songs,
I praise and worship God, tears on my face!

Praise God for this revelation to me,
Salvation is promised, when God's at work,
One day, full fruitfulness for prayers, we'll see!

When God's in control, our battles are won,
His strength given to us each day we pray,
Till victory comes, our life purpose done!

Seeking God

Our desire to see God changes our life;
Pursuing the Lord helps overcome strife;

We must not worry about food, drink, clothes
Just trust in God's goodness; our needs He knows!

Rejecting evil, turning toward good,
We want to please God, as we know we should.

With eyes open, seeking God with clean heart,
Our faith blossoms, confidence to impart!

"*But seek first his kingdom and his righteousness, and all these things* (food, drink, clothes) *will be given to you as well*" (Mathew 6:33).

Solitude: What Is It?

Solitude is confidence, trusting one's own heart to be true,
To do what is right, to follow love's path, to believe joy's dew
Will fall, just as the promises of God are always faithful,
And God's Presence stays watchful, never leaves us, always wakeful!

Solitude is not loneliness, but the opposite of this,
As contemplation renews the soul, a satisfying bliss
Received as ears open to hear words of hope, reviving life,
And minds grasp truth's power to carve disease and sin out, with knife.

Solitude seeks beauty, the loveliness of a waterfall,
Recollections sweet, days gone by, walking through memories' hall;
Thanksgiving and rejoicing, bubbling up like a fountain,
Answered prayers seen, grateful hearts now a voice, climbing joy's mountain.

Solitude lights entrance into place where true love can abide,
Quietness and trust envelope couples, honeymooner's bride
Enjoying belonging's embrace, feeling cherished, and in love,
Trusting heart's covenant bond, believing love's words from above.

Twenty Words

Twenty words, Lord,
containing the gospel in a nutshell:
Help us to love God and love one another,
in the love that God gives for ourselves and one another.
Twenty words, Lord,
protecting us and all we know from hell:
Help us to love God and love one another,
in the love that God gives for ourselves and one another.
Twenty words, Lord,
empowering joyful heart's mighty swell:
Help us to love God and love one another,
in the love that God gives for ourselves and one another.
Twenty words, Lord,
expanding Your kingdom, faith to compel!

Thank You, Lord, for giving us love today,
Thank You for giving us Your thoughts to pray.

"Jesus replied, "'Love the Lord your God with all your heart and with all your soul and with all your mind." This is the first and greatest commandment. And the second is like it; "Love your neighbour as yourself." All the Law and the Prophets hang on these two commandments'" (Matthew 22:37–40).

Vision's Footsteps

make me able to see and pray with fresh eyes, and fresh "i" choices
insight's footsteps made into fifteen VISIONS, VESPERS, and VOICES

    insights   illuminations
       ideas   instruments
           images   inheritance
         inspirations   intersessions
             impressions   instructions
                                                                  interests
                illustrations   intentions
                       imagination
                     interpretations

Inspiration for theme of "vespers, visions, voices" came from Nancy (Warwick) Kingdon's earlier published book of poetry, *Humming Words: A Collection of Poetry* (2018).

Chapter 2
Authority

TABLE OF CONTENTS

Beware Bitter Roots	18
Contemplating Part 1: God's Seven Promises to Jacob	19
Contemplating Part 2: Jacob's Seven Responses to God	20
Contemplating The New Covenant: Part 1	22
Contemplating The New Covenant: Part 2	23
Emergency Numbers: The Traveller's Psalm	24
God's Growth Promises	25
Hospitality's Power	26
Perfumed Vessels	27
Purposefully Rewarded	28
Shocking Authority: Part 1	29
Shocking Authority: Part 2	30
Tree of Life Called Wisdom: Parts 1, 2 and 3	31
Trusting God Through Change	34
Word of God	35

Themes in this chapter include authority, Word of God, promises, revelation.

Beware Bitter Roots

Submit yourself to divine will, trusting God;
Acknowledge His goodness and sovereignty
To want only what's best, not wrath's cruel rod.

Beware bitter roots that can stay hidden
From view and yet pollute thinking patterns
To cause lies, accepting what's forbidden.

Bitterness, like dregs in a vat of wine
Can contaminate and sour whole batch
Till useless, like rinds tossed out to swine.

Rejection, disappointments, envy, strife
Can cause bitter roots to begin to grow,
As can anger at death of dear one's life.

What do you do if you have bitter roots?
You must repent, asking God for mercy!
Seek forgiveness; pray for holiness's shoots!

"Repent," Peter tells sorcerer named
Simon: "I see you are captive to sin
And full of bitterness," Peter declares.

Grace gardens or bitter roots—it's our choice
One path leads to fruitfulness and fullness,
Other to sadness, disappointment's voice.

Inspiration for this poem came from sermon preached by Rev. Rick Busse, Lead Pastor, Evangel Church, Oshawa Ontario on June 23, 2024. See Acts 8:22–23.

"Make every effort to live in peace with everyone and to be holy; without holiness no one will see the Lord. See to it that no one falls short of the grace of God and that no bitter root grows up to cause trouble and defile man" (Hebrews 12:14–15).

Contemplating, Part 1:
God's Seven Promises to Jacob

In Genesis 28 we read about Jacob's Dream at Bethel
Putting a stone under his head, he lay down to sleep, and he dreamed
Of a staircase connecting earth to heaven, with angels ascending
And descending; above staircase stood the Lord, who said, "I am the Lord,
The God of your father Abraham and the God of Isaac, I am."

God's **First promise** to Jacob**:** "The ground you're lying on belongs to you;
I'm giving it to you!" said the God of Jacob, Abraham, Isaac.
God's **second promise** was to declare that Jacob's descendants be blessed.
"Your descendants will be like the dust of the earth, and you will spread out to
The west, the east, the north, and the south; they will multiply and spread out!
Then, God's **third promise**: "And all the peoples of the earth will be blessed
through you and your offspring." All your descendants will be greatly blessed!
God proclaimed His **fourth promise** to not leave him, saying, "I am with you;"
I will never leave you nor forsake you, God promised Jacob's offspring.
Fifthly, God promised to protect him, saying, "I will watch over you
 Wherever you go." I will watch over you and protect you always.
Sixthly, God promised to bring him back to this land, returning someday.
And finally, God's **seventh promise** was that He would never leave him
until all His gracious words were fulfilled for Jacob, just as promised!

See Jacob's Dream at Bethel, described in Genesis 28:10–22.

Inspiration for this poem came when the author noticed seven responses from Jacob to God's seven promises; since this was a fresh insight, it intrigued Nancy enough to write this poem and the one that follows.

Contemplating, Part 2:
Jacob's Seven Responses to God

Jacob had a dream. He saw a stairway resting on the earth, with its top reaching to heaven, and the angels of God were ascending and descending on it. There above it, God stood, ready to speak seven promises.

Jacob awoke from his sleep and said, "Surely the Lord is in this place, and I was not aware of it"—thus proclaiming God's Presence.
Jacob's **first response** to God's first promise is **acknowledgement of God.**

Secondly, Jacob exhibits reverence, fear of the Lord, and awe,
Saying, "How awesome is this place! This is none other than the house of God; this is the gate to heaven." Jacob's second response is **reverence!**

Thirdly, seeing God's blessing, Jacob **takes action!** The next morning Jacob got up early;
he took the stone he had rested his head against, setting it upright as a memorial pillar.

Fourthly, **worship** was in Jacob's heart when he poured oil over the stone.

Fifthly, Jacob **names the place** where He met God. "He called the place Bethel" (which means 'house of God'), though the city used to be called Luz."

Sixthly, Jacob vows the Lord will be his God, saying, "If God will be with me and will watch over me on this journey I am taking and will give me food to eat and clothes to wear, so that I return safely to my father's household, then **the Lord will be my God.**"

Seventhly, Jacob responds with a **vow to tithe**, as an act of worship, saying, "And this stone that I have set up as a pillar will be God's house, and of all that you give me I will give you a tenth."

Jacob's dream at Bethel highlights both seven promises of God and Jacob's seven heart responses to God's gracious blessings to him and his offspring.

See Jacob's Dream at Bethel in Genesis 28:10–22 and read note on Contemplating, Part 1.

Contemplating The New Covenant
Part 1

"I will put my laws in their minds," declares the Lord,
"I will write them on their hearts," not on stone tablets;
Later, *"I will put my laws in their hearts and I
Will write them on their minds,"* forgiving all their sins.
Both hearts and minds are storage containers, holding
Laws of truth in perfect balance with divine grace;
How awesome to contemplate the New Covenant
Reconciling human hearts with our Holy God!

Read Jeremiah 31:33; Hebrews 8:10, 16.

Contemplating The New Covenant
Part 2

Thank You, Lord, for Your Word, Your Way, and Your Wisdom,
Teaching us to ponder Your promises and love.
What does it look like—to know the love of Jesus,
Stored in holy vessels, flowing through flesh tablets?
Hebrews ten, verses twenty-two to thirty-nine
Tell us seven measurable outcomes, or signs:

- you will draw nearer to God, with a sincere heart
- you will hold unswervingly to hope you profess
- you will spur one another to love and good deeds
- you will not give up meeting together, praying
- you will increase encouraging one another
- you will persevere daily, pursuing God's will
- you will live by faith, always seeking righteousness

Help us, dear God, to receive Your new covenant!

Read Hebrews 10:22–39.

Emergency Numbers:
The Traveller's Psalm

Whether starting an adventure,
Facing hardship or loving life,
Psalm one-twenty-one is a song
For people on a pilgrimage!

We learn: our Creator helps us;
He watches over us always!
As Protector, He does not sleep;
Forever, He keeps us from harm!

I lift up my eyes to the mountains—
where does my help come from?
My help comes from the Lord,
the Maker of heaven and earth.

He will not let your foot slip—
he who watches over you will not slumber;
indeed, he who watches over you
will neither slumber nor sleep.

The Lord watches over you—
the Lord is your shade at your right hand;
the sun will not harm you by day,
nor the moon by night.

The Lord will keep you from all harm—
he will watch over your life;
the Lord will watch over your coming and going,
both now and forevermore.
(Psalm 121:1–8)

God's Growth Promises

God's
7
GROWTH
PROMISES

Protection

Provision

Prayers

Purposes

Passions

Peace

Power

Hospitality's Power

Did you know Jesus used food to resolve conflicts?
Doubting Thomas joined Him to dine;
Peter ate fish Jesus roasted over fire pits.

Hospitality has power to bring healings;
Relationships can get mended
When Love restores brokenness and heals hurt feelings.

Like Peter, we are asked to feed God's lambs and sheep,
Showing hospitality to all,
Praying for healed-heart's reconciliation sweep!

Even prickly-pear personalities can heal,
From rejection, from brokenness's pain
Set free—old wounds tossed like a banana peel!

Why not invite someone to sit down, food eating
For your next difficult challenge,
And Satan's plans to divide, you'll be defeating!

Read John 20:24, 21:12, 15–17

Inspiration for this poem came from a discussion on the principles of biblical leadership on March 27, 2024 at Clarington's monthly CCBF Breakfast, on the topic of "Priorities and Purposes of Life."

My husband, Rod Kingdon, talked about the biblical principle of choosing to break bread, or share a meal with someone, if there is a difficult, challenging matter to resolve, instead of a phone call or office visit.

Perfumed Vessels

Spending time in God's Presence, worshipping, fills us
with renewed love, restores our faith, and refreshes,
empowering us to become vessels for God's love
To flow through, with enough surplus to give away;

Praying, seeking God's Presence daily, keeps us strong
In faith, enabling us to receive God's love
in increasing measure, in growing abundance,
God's grace expanding our capacity to love!

Reading and praying God's Word aloud opens hearts
To know God's desires better, and what pleases Him,
Teaching us to obey His Word and be blessed
With deeper grasp of love's encompassing essence!

Only vessels emptied of pride and cleansed within
Have the desire to pursue God, adoring Him
With praises, worship, and a heart of devotion;
Seeking to breath in then breath out love's perfumed essence!

Purposefully Rewarded

P   Power belongs to God
U   Unfailing love is His;
R   Rewards come
P   Purposefully
O   One to one given
S   Such gifts to
E   Everyone rewarded

    F
        U
            L
                L
                    Y
                  according to
                  what they have done!

"One thing God has spoken, two things I have heard: 'Power belongs to you, God, and with you, Lord, is unfailing love'; and, 'You reward everyone according to what they have done'" (Psalm 62:11–12).

Shocking Authority
Part 1

Shocking
Authority found
in Jesus' Words of life;
Startling　　　　Authority
Empowered　to　combat
Strife;　Star　lit　Authority
Searches hearts and minds with knife
To cut out　damage,　erase　bitterness
Healing released—lives soaring to wholeness
Securely wrapped　in　Jesus'　Words　of life!

Inspiration: God's authority is shocking! It's so far beyond what we can imagine if we accept and believe God's Word and His Promises that as His disciples, empowered by God's Spirit, we will be able to do what Jesus has done, and even more.

"'Have faith in God,' Jesus answered. 'Truly I tell you if anyone says to this mountain, "Go, throw yourself into the sea," and does not doubt in their heart but believes that what they say will happen, it will be done for them. Therefore, I tell you, whatever you ask for in prayer, believe that you have received it, and it will be yours'" (Mark 11:22–24).

Shocking Authority
Part 2

Prayer changes everything
Making hearts dance and sing!
When Jesus is named Lord
God's Word becomes a sword;
Slicing through strongholds of sin,
Melting bitterness within.
Shocking authority empowers nations to be healed!
God's promises and authority's answered prayers revealed!

"*If my people, who are called by my name, will humble themselves and pray and seek my face and turn from their wicked ways, then I will hear from heaven, and I will forgive their sin and will heal their land*" (2 Chronicles 7:14).

Tree of Life Called Wisdom
Part 1

Happy
is the man
who finds wisdom,
and the man who gets
understanding, for the
gain
from it is better than gain from
silver and its profit better than gold.
She is more precious than jewels,
and nothing you desire can
compare with
her.
Long life is in her right hand; in her left hand are
riches and honor. Her ways are ways of pleasantness,
and all her paths are peace. She is a
tree of life

Proverbs 3:13–18a, RSV

Tree of Life called Wisdom
Part 2

Joyful
is
the person
who finds wisdom,
the one who gains
understanding. For
wisdom
is more profitable
than silver, and her wages are
better
than gold.

Wisdom is more
precious
than rubies;

nothing you desire can compare
with her. She
(Wisdom)
offers you long life
in her right hand and riches
and honor in her left. She will
guide
you down
delightful paths; all her ways
are satisfying Wisdom is a

tree of life

Proverbs 3:13–18a, NLT

Tree of Life called Wisdom
Part 3

Blessed
are those
who finds wisdom,
those who gain understanding,
for
she is
more profitable than silver
and yields better returns than gold.
She
is more precious
than rubies; nothing
you desire can compare with her.
Long
life is in
her right hand; in her
left hand are riches and honor.
Her
ways are
pleasant ways,
and all her paths are peace.
She
is a tree of life.

Proverbs 3:13–18a

Trusting God Through Change

In God I trust! In my unchanging God,
I trust! I trust! I trust! Now and always!

I walk through all trials and changes in life,
with my hand in the hand of my Jesus,

who guides me and leads me in a straight path
of righteousness, opening all closed doors,

and closing doors that are not right for me
when my purpose is to glorify God!

Nothing is impossible when God leads,
And unfurls winds through roaring, changing seas!

God can quiet the winds with one command:
"Be still!," and all of creation listens!

Praise the Lord, O my soul, praise Jesus' name!
The One who saves, delivers and rules all!

Amen

Inspiration for this poem came from the theme message of the draft of my memoir, which is "navigating change."

Word of God

W   Wisdom: I'm asking for wisdom from God's Spirit.
O   Opening Minds, God's Word inside ears now heard!
R   Revelation I crave, seeing with passionate vision
D   Discernment giving hearts God's true compassion!

How can God's Word give such powerful insight?
How can God's Word unfold such heartfelt delight?
A mystery—God's Holy Spirit ALIVE
In us, God's Word sparking our hearts to revive!

"If any of you lacks wisdom, you should ask God, who gives generously to all without finding fault, and it will be given to you. But when you ask, you must believe and not doubt, because the one who doubts is like a wave of the sea, blown and tossed by the wind" (James 1:5–6).

"The fruit of the righteous is a tree of life, and the one who is wise saves lives" (Proverbs 11:30).

"Blessed are those who find wisdom, those who gain understanding, for she is more profitable than silver and yields better returns than gold. She is more precious than rubies; nothing you desire can compare with her" (Proverb 3:13 –15).

Chapter 3

Inheritance

TABLE OF CONTENTS

Building Bible College Capacity	38
Celebrating ESL Ministry Launch	40
God Is Love	42
God's Inheritance	43
Grow Your Church Today, Dear God	44
Growth Track Steps	45
Healing Place	46
Launching ESL Ministry	47
Limitlessness	48
Love-Empowered Offspring	51
Maggie's Place Beckons: Come!	52
Meet Magnolia Maggie	54
Powerful Prayer of Unquantifiable Love	56
We Are Your Fruit	58
You Are My Beloved	59

Themes in this chapter include inheritance, church, and the restored church, called Magnolia Maggie.

Building Bible College Capacity

Today, dear friend, let's support a Bible college,
Creating CAP-A-CITY to function short-term
And flourish long-term, equipping with excellence
New church leaders, disciples, and missionaries,
Expanding God's kingdom on earth as in heaven.

What key issues face many Bible colleges?
Shrinking enrollment cuts revenue to function;
Distance learning has grown through COVID's influence;
Donor fatigue creates stress as costs escalate;
Declining church attendance means less prayer support.

What can we do to help our Bible colleges?
First, pray, pray, pray for leadership and student needs;
Second, promote college to prospective students;
Third, sacrificially give, increasing support;
Fourth, ask God to send workers into the harvest.

There's a formula for most Bible colleges:
Thirty per cent of revenue comes from donors,
Twenty per cent from rentals, dorms, food services,
Fifty per cent, student enrollment and class hours.
Can you give, send a student, or offer prayers?

Master's College has launched a new teaching model
To invite local churches to become node sites,
Bringing college learning into church families,
Where mentoring of our young people can flourish,
And future leaders will be nourished from within!

May God now raise up ears to hear His heart's desire,
For all of us to think about tomorrow's church
And need to equip future pastoral leaders
And need to pray for God's favour on colleges—
Thus expanding God's will on earth as in heaven!

Inspiration: The author has served as an ABHE Evaluator Team member at half a dozen Bible colleges across North American, and now recognizes that most Bible colleges desperately need a stronger ongoing church support base. They also need increased enrollment to confidently balance budgets, and to better fulfill their call to equip future leaders for ministry and evangelism needs.

Our PAOC Bible colleges NEED the support of the church family to not merely survive but thrive! In 2024, a new PAOC initiative has been launched to encourage local churches to partner as training centres and site locations for biblical learning. Please pray about your role in this kingdom-building opportunity!

Celebrating ESL Ministry Launch

After a community survey
Identifying ESL need,
And much prayer seeking God's will and plan,
God opened doors and began **to MOVE** …
ESL Ministry was launched
In Fall two thousand and twenty-three
At Evangel Church in Oshawa
Using Bible-based curriculum
From LIGHT OF THE WORLD training centre;
Step one was training ten volunteers
Method of MODEL-REPEAT-SOLO
Style of LOTW lesson plans;
All volunteers committed to teach
Twenty-eight lessons with new students.
Step two was setting up classroom space
Tables and television needed
For three classrooms as students signed up
for lesson one, beginner's level
Offered to our first nineteen students.
Team teaching is our preferred model
To allow occasional absence
Of a volunteer from weekly class;
At seven weeks, students are tested,
Celebrating how much they've learned
Delighting in their new confidence
Speaking conversational English!
Step three has been having team meetings
To encourage our refreshment team,
Helpers, and teachers to connect
And share ideas, progress, and prayers
For our students and ongoing needs.

Step four is the growth in attendance—
Now seventy students have joined us
From eleven different nations!
Students have started coming to church,
Some asking to be baptized, and some
Joining the assembly as partners,
Bringing their children and families
Out to church functions and ministries.
PRAISE GOD for this amazing blessing
Of seeing God at work, **MOVING FAST!**
And giving much cause to celebrate!
May God's will be done in all these lives
And may God continue to strengthen
Our team and our students through His love
Drawing us close, into His Presence
And into belonging's family!

Inspiration: The author has been a part of the ESL Ministry launch at Evangel Church in Oshawa since 2023 and is grateful for the MOVE of God that has brought such amazing people to our church, and such fruitfulness and blessing. To God be the glory, for these great things He has done!

God Is Love

This day God reminded me of three words
I wrote on my brother's black typewriter
cover, bold red nail polish proclaiming:
GOD IS LOVE! Script from past—life sustaining!

It's time to know and rely on God's love!
Why? because GOD IS LOVE and GOD SPARKS LOVE!
These are the best three words in history,
The best three words in everyone's story!

Your best legacy will be these three words,
Spoken to your children and grandchildren:
Today, tell them: GOD IS LOVE! Show them, too
How you've been changed, heart transformed---brand new!

"And so we know and rely on the love God has for us. God is love. Whoever lives in love lives in God, and God in them" (1 John 4:16).

God's Inheritance

God loves you, delights in you; over you He'll dance!
Are you aware that you are God's inheritance?
Love released is such a powerful advantage—
It transforms all in its path; minds and hearts it'll change,
From feeling rejected to knowing belonging,
Healing power satisfying every longing
Is ours, when we submit in love to God above,
Believing in Him, knowing Him—then He'll approve
Who we have become, by God's grace at work in us.

Now acknowledged as a child of God, thrust thus
Beyond all that we could imagine or have dreamed
Possible, but not outside His grace, now esteemed
Through our voices, our testimonies of great things
Done by God, through floods released, as great grace He brings!

Grow Your Church Today, Dear God

Grow Your Church today, Dear God, today
              Scattering words of faith as seed's might

Grow Your Church today, Dear God, today
              Watering plants, with love as power

Grow Your Church today, Dear God, today
              Radiating hope, as shining light

Grow Your Church today, Dear God, today
              Blossoming joyfulness as bright flower

Growth Track Steps

When you authentically LOVE people,
Grace circles spread, throwing strong, wide ripples

When churches foster SAFE community,
Inside, see belonging's identity!

When your heart seeks and encounters JESUS,
Expect hope, joy, peace—abundant life plus!

When you choose to experience PURPOSE,
Spiritual gifts will flow through Jesus!

Inspiration for this poem came from mission-vision-goals of Evangel Pentecostal Church in Oshawa, Ontario.

Healing Place

Everyone, EVERYWHERE, empowered
To receive healing from God, wisdom and revelation flowing,
Proclaiming the power of Jesus to heal hearts, heal lands, heal nations
Through the Church He delights in, the Church He calls as His inheritance!

Come! You are invited to the healing place!
Come! Today receive God's forgiveness and grace!
 Prayer overflows hearts with oneness' embrace!
Oneness, Spiritual Oneness discovered!

E	Everyone
V	Victorious,
E	Empowered!
R	Released!
Y	Yearning for
W	Wisdom,
H	Healing
E	Embraced!
R	Revelation
E	Encountered

Inspired by Ephesians 1:7–23 and 2 Chronicles 7:14, which reads: *"If my people, who are called by my name, will humble themselves and pray and seek my face and turn from their wicked ways, then I will hear from heaven and I will forgive their sin and will heal their land."*

This poem was read aloud by the author on November 3, 2024 to celebrate the official launch of Evangel Church's new name, which changed from "Evangel" to "Healing Place."

Launching ESL Ministry

thank You, Lord, for ESL
      English learning done so well
           church ministries so bright.

each one, teach one,
      language learning excitement
           to read, speak, understand, write.

each one, reach one,
      gospel message with love sent
           lifting hearts to great height.

each one preach one,
      Word of God, scripture verses
           feeding minds on truth's insight.

may new heart's awakening
      end hurts, deception's aching,
           righting wrongs, as faith takes flight!

Inspiration for this poem came from an ESL teacher training workshop held for fifteen volunteers in 2024 at Evangel Church in Oshawa.

Limitlessness

Your WORD is a Door
W O R D
O   O
R   O
D O O R

O P E N
P
E
N
O P E N

OPEN
to
receive
MY HEART
ENTERING

Inside
is a ROOM
wrapped
in
wonder
painted walls,
colours bright,
amazing
images,
poems,
ideas,
insight
into
rainbow skies;
promises given,

answers of why
removes all doubt;
how, what, when,
where forgotten;
lost in WHO
beckons

me
inside
this room;
invites me
to gaze in
wonder;
to see
love
endlessly unfolding revelations and wisdom beyond measure;
limitless possibilities released as perfume, as poetry, as praises;
unstoppable, victorious, declared and therefore released into
light …
elation's
formation, a
trans-form-ation
impacting all of creation!
WHO has infinite power
to make   a difference
to change our world.
love's the answer,
healing nation
through
love's
WHEEL
a
W O R D
H   R
E   I
E   V
L O V E

a word drive,
a love wheel,
patterning sky
like
stars
sparkling
with truth
forever!

Love-Empowered Offspring

Who is God?   God is LOVE!

        Who are you?   You are God's   o   offspring,
                                 You are God's   I   inheritance,
                                 You are God's   l   love Song.
                                 You are God's
                                              LAMP   God's oil lamp
                                              love-lit identity!

Who is God?   God is WHOLENESS!

        Who are you?   You are God's   d   design plan,
                                 You are His   r   restoration project,
                                 You are the   e   embrace of God's heart,
                                 You are the   a   apple of God's eye,
                                 You are His   m   masterpiece of art.

Who is God?   God is OUR SOURCE OF EVERY GOOD GIFT!

        Who are you?   You are God's DREAM COME TRUE
                               empowered with His Spirit's OIL of gladness,
                               to seek to know and love God!

"Every good and perfect gift is from above, coming down from the Father of the heavenly lights, who does not change like shifting shadows" (James 1:17).

Maggie's Place Beckons: Come!

I dream of the church transformed, empowered love's light;
What is her name, this song in God's heart, His delight?

Magnolia Maggie is what He calls His Bride;
Her beauty, Her heart of love, Her fragrance, His pride.

A vessel she is, a place of mercy and grace,
Overflowing with peace, there's a smile on her face.

As she welcomes into her arms all who have need
Of prayer, of love, of mercy's magnificent seed,

A garden of love's promise, undeserving grace,
Yet her beauty comes from eyes fixed on Jesus' face.

She's a church, a bride prepared to receive God's love,
Thus, able to worship, she sends true love above;

She's a lighthouse, shining with belonging's grace root,
Mercy and grace glowing identity's sweet fruit.

Maggie's Place beckons, COME! Here you'll find answered prayer,
Not 'cause of us, but because of God's divine care!

She's a door, a place of prayer, a heart forgiven,
And, therefore, magnanimous grace is now given;

She loves all who walk into her friendly embrace;
COME TODAY! God's love is released in MAGGIE'S PLACE!

God's AIM: Alive In Mercy, found in MAGGIE'S PLACE!
God's GEM: Grace Empowered Mercy, joy's sparkling face!

Alive in Mercy, surely God's desire for all;
Listening ears of transformed hearts will hear God's call.

Grace Empowered Mercy, is that joy on your face?
Come today! God's love is released in MAGGIE'S PLACE!

Inspiration: Around 2007, Nancy (Warwick) Kingdon, the writer of this poem, heard in her spirit the name "Magnolia Maggie" as God's name for His Redeemed Church; that's why she feels that she can call the restored church "Maggie's Place."

Meet Magnolia Maggie

Some years ago, a white stone was given to me.
On it, I heard aloud the name for God's healed church:
Magnolia Maggie, perfumed with mercy free,
Flowing mercy, sins erased, not found after search;
She arose rejoicing, a daughter, full of grace,
Her thankful heart overflowing, knowing God's face!

If grace causes hearts to forgive, mercy forgets
That the sin ever happened, that the hurt took place;
Mercy instead sees all others free from all debts,
No payment needed, no judgement coming, just grace.
Belonging's dignity is served; gracious cup
Not tearing down but building one another up!

After all, God sees each one of us without sin,
If we believe in Jesus' sacrifice for all,
If we turn to Him, acknowledging His great win
Cut from sin's hold, we can answer His divine call,
To love God and love others as our central goal;
God's new covenant releasing each hurt, lost soul!

Magnolia Maggie has her straight path cut out;
But she will be judged for only one thing alone:
Did she BELIEVE in Jesus, thanksgiving her shout?
Did she accept her new name, written on white stone?
Knowing she's forgiven, did others she forgive?
As her thank offering, her perfumed gift to give?

That sweet fragrance of forgiveness floats everywhere
Magnolia Maggie, God's workmanship, does go;
As Spirit of God moves, answering sincere prayer,
Beautiful breezes of belonging's voice will blow
Into desperate places, hope for God's adored!
Mercy And Grace, Grace Intentionally Explored!

Perfumed magnolia blooms, blushing white
Scent secret landscape's passionate desire
To see God's family honoured, made right
Pleasing His heart, healed by holy fire
Consuming deep within hearts raging sin,
Freeing her to arise, new heart within!

Inspiration: Listening to a sermon on July 24, 2022, I was reminded of my secret inner heart's name for the restored church, which I call *Magnolia Maggie.*

Paul's prayer in Acts 20:32 is relevant for believers today: *"Now I commit you to God and the word of his grace, which can build you up and give you an inheritance among all those who are sanctified."*

Powerful Prayer of Unquantifiable Love

If you pray over your loved ones, yourself, and your church family
Paul's prayer in Ephesians 3, you'll have poured out blessings so great,
So amazing, so abundant, there's not enough room to hold all!

Paul celebrates that through faith in Christ Jesus, we can approach God
In freedom and full confidence. *"For this reason I kneel before
the Father, from whom every family in heaven and earth
derives its name. I pray that out of his glorious riches he may
strengthen you with power through his Spirit in your inner being,
so that Christ may dwell in your hearts through faith."* Thus, God's identity
Is given to us, His children, His family, called by His name!

Let's pray, with Paul, his next blessing: *"And I pray that you, being rooted
and established in love, may have power, together with all the
Lord's holy people, to grasp how wide and long and high and deep is
the love of Christ, and to know this love that surpasses knowledge—that
you may be filled to all the measure of all the fullness of
God. Now to him who is able to do immeasurably more
than all we ask or imagine, according to his power that
is at work within us, to him be glory in the church and in
Christ Jesus throughout all generations for ever and ever."*

Amen! Think of a tree, established in love, rooted, growing tall,
Empowered to grasp the essence of unquantifiable love,
That can be entered, and in so doing can be like a river,
Filling a heart beyond measure, even to the fullness of God!
That kind of love has limitless power, surpassing all knowledge!
And since it glorifies Christ Jesus, there can be no higher prayer,
And no greater blessing for you, your loved ones, and your church, than this!

Scripture quotations in this poem came from Ephesians 3: 14–21.

Inspiration for this poem came from a sermon on Ephesians 3 preached by Rev. Chris Canning at Evangel Pentecostal Church, Oshawa, Ontario on August 6, 2023.

We Are Your Fruit

Investing in the next generation is not optional;
It's mandatory!
Becoming God's "inheritance" and even His "love letter,"
Revealing God's love,
As His Spirit works in us and through us, will glorify God.

Imagine how you'd feel if a group of young people told you:
"We are your fruit!"
Wouldn't it make your heart feel proud as you look at their faith walk
And see godliness
As they seek to become disciples and disciple-makers?

Are you committed to having a mentor, and a mentee?
Relationships count
In the kingdom of God and in advancing leadership skills;
It's time to listen
To God's call to mentor and be mentored as disciples.

Inspiration for this poem came from reading Geninne Bridge's contribution to *We the Called. Mobilizing a Mentoring Movement*:

> "We are your fruit." These were the words of my youth in Pickering Ont, celebrating as I transitioned out of pastoral ministry into district ministry. Those words were the culmination of why mentoring matters and why investing in the next generation through discipleship pathways is required for the body of Christ to accomplish its call of teaching others the hope we have in Jesus Christ.[3]

---

[3] Geninne Bridge in *We the Called. Mobilizing a Mentoring Movement*, David Wells and Rich Janes, Eds. (Mississauga, ON: The Pentecostal Assemblies of Canada, 2024), 41–42.

You Are My Beloved

Have I told You today, dear One,
You are my RADIANCE of joy!

> Have I told You today, dear *(insert your name)*,
> How much I love You? I love You!
> I love You! I REALLY love You!

Have I told You today, dear Friend,
You are my MASTERPIECE of peace!

> Have I told You today, dear *(insert your name)*,
> How much I love You? I love You!
> I love You! I REALLY love You!

Have I told You today, dear Child,
You are my HEART'S RIVER of love!

> Have I told You today, dear (insert your name),
> How much I love You? I love You!
> I love You! I REALLY love You!

Have I told You, today, dear Heart,
You are my FAITH FLOWER of hope!

> Have I told You today, dear *(insert your name)*,
> How much I love You? I love You!
> I love You! I REALLY love You!

Inspiration for this poem came from a suggestion from a friend of mine, Rev. Laurence Van Kleek, retired library director at Summit Pacific Bible College in Abbottsford, British Columbia. He suggested that I prepare God's response of how much He loves each one of us, as a mirrored message and a companion to my earlier poem "You are My Cornerstone."[4]

---

[4] Nancy Kingdon, "You Are My Cornerstone," in *Arising Rejoicing: A Collection of Devotional Poetry* (Meadville, PA: Christian Faith Publishing, 2023), 51.

Chapter 4
Transformation

TABLE OF CONTENTS

Abiding's Embrace (song)	62
Blessings Poured Out	63
Breath of Life Celebrated	64
Come, Holy Spirit!	65
Each One Caring	66
Easter's Story	67
Flowing River of Life	68
Fruit of the Spirit	69
Gratitude's Heart Song	70
Healing Our Land	71
In Your Presence	72
Life's Greatest Question	73
Wedding of the Lamb	74
Wisdom's Path	75
Zesty Fruit of the Spirit	76

Themes in this chapter include transformation and forgiveness.

Abiding's Embrace
(song)

A	Abiding—a gloriously bright word,
B	Blessed rejoicing's voice, like joy's songbird
I	Inside God's Presence, delightful pleasure;
D	Dwelling place filled with praise beyond measure,
I	Illuminating happiness heart's home,
N	Nourishing faithfulness's roots till full grown
G	Grace forests arise, ABIDING'S EMBRACE!

Refrain:
ABIDING's faithful embrace—
homecoming's call from above
Inviting us to enter
grace forests of endless love!

Blessings Poured Out

Overflowing with belonging's goodness,
Our Heavenly Father's heart is so big
He welcomes, cherishes, and invites all
To become His child, His inheritance,
Created to bless, just as He blesses,
Created to love, just as He loves all.

Welcomed into God's family of joy,
Forgiven of all wrongdoings and sins,
And able to give others forgiveness
Beyond limits, through God's merciful grace,
So that belonging's goodness flows freely
Through wounded hearts, separated from hope.

Grace, like a river of refreshment, flows,
Paying it forward, healing broken hearts
With Father God's embrace of belonging,
And through His children's gift of forgiveness,
Blessings poured out from hearts of thanksgiving;
Blessings beyond measure released, poured forth!

Breath of Life Celebrated

Breath of life, beautiful breath of air, I welcome You!
Savouring belonging's peace, I say, "Hello, adieu."
Holy Breath, I inhale fragrance, Your beauty I know;
As breath by breath falls softly, majestic flakes of snow
Covering my inner landscape with thanksgiving's grace
Filling memory's halls with smiles lighting up each face.

How often I take each breath for granted, all day long,
Forgetting to thank God for His gift, His grace song.
That gives not only physical well-being and joy
But offers spiritual dividends to enjoy,
As I invite God's Holy Spirit into my heart,
Alive at last, joy set free, transformation's new start!

Come, Holy Spirit!

Come, Holy Spirit! Precious Jesus, Come!
Come, Holy Father; Creator, Welcome!
Come today, our Redeemer and Healer,
Transform our land, our cities, Canada!
Restore our churches and our families!

Come! Teach us Your ways, instruct and bless us,
To be equipped to do Your will, Your way;
Grant us Your favour and deliverance;
Empty us of ourselves and then fill us
With Your authority, power, and grace!

Each One Caring

Each one reaching and teaching others, empowering arts!
Each one learning what it means to live among caring hearts!

E	Exploring courageous servant leadership choices,
A	As justice and kindness are mankind's mantle voices;
C	Creating cathedral heart spaces—awe and worship,
H	Holding hands, caring hearts building communities grand!
E	Each leader's hope inspiring mercy's scope,
A	Always kind, caring, always just, daring;
C	Communities giving gracious living,
H	Hope reaching out, fighting unbelief's doubt

Each one reaching and teaching others, empowering grace!
Each one learning how to create awe's cathedral heart space!

Inspiration for this poem came from viewing a short video on Living Waters' website, as resort owner Larry Law was awarded the prestigious Chinese Canadian Entrepreneurship award for 2021–2022.

"Jesus had compassion on them and touched their eyes. Immediately they received their sight and followed him" (Mathew 20:34).

Easter's Story

Jesus' resurrection victory
    Is our joyful Easter story;
God's living Word
    Spoken and heard;
Praise to our Lord
    Voices in accord;
Lighting our path
    Defeating sin's wrath;
New covenant
    Creation's fresh chant;
Enlightened heart
    Sabbath Rest joy start;
Jesus' resurrection victory
    Is today's joyful Easter glory!

"For anyone who enters God's rest also rests from their works, just as God did from his. Let us, therefore, make every effort to enter that rest, so that no one will perish by following their example of disobedience" (Hebrews 4:10–11).

Flowing River of Life

F	Freedom's flight begins with turning away from sin,
L	Like a flowing river of life, hope to begin;
O	Opening hearts to heal, minds to understand how
W	Wisdom's work produces deliverance to show
I	Illuminated patience, gentleness, and love,
N	Not naturally produced, but grace from above,
G	Guiding healing from humanity's brokenness!

F   Flowing grace will carry healing river of
    L   Life forward, even to the ends of the earth!
        O
           W
              I
                 N
                    G

Flowing,
    Flowing,
        Flowing grace,
            Flowing forward,   forward,   forward … … …

"*A person's wisdom yields patience; it is to one's glory to overlook an offense*" (Proverbs 19:11).

"*The fear of the Lord leads to life; then one rests content, untouched by trouble*" (Proverbs 19: 21).

Fruit of the Spirit

Dear God,
I ASK YOU TO …
form-reform-unform-inform-transform
as needed, TILL YOUR
F R U I T
of the Spirit
grows in me, unhindered
grows in us, without barrier;
empowered to do Your will,
free from desires not of You,
equipped to serve You in Your plans and anointing,
Increasing love, joy, peace, forbearance, kindness,
goodness, faithfulness, gentleness, and self-control!

"But the fruit of the Spirit is love, joy, peace, forbearance, kindness, goodness, faithfulness, gentleness and self-control. Against such things there is no law. Those who belong to Christ Jesus have crucified the flesh with its passions and desires. Since we live by the Spirit, let us keep in step with the Spirit" (Galatians 5:22–24).

Gratitude's Heart Song

Lord, may all that we do, think, say, and pray
Be done from hearts of gratitude today!

Your compassion we desire, dear Jesus;
Teach us to respond in love, dear Jesus;
Open our eyes to see through Your heart's love;
Give us ears to know God's voice from above.

We rejoice today in Your salvation!
Thanksgiving's now our heart's motivation,
As we think about all that You have done:
To give us Jesus—Your beloved Son!

Lord, may all that we do, think, say, and pray
Be done from hearts of gratitude today!

Healing Our Land

Cultural and spiritual transformation
will be possible only through a move of God!

To be a FORCEFUL catalyst for revival,
You must daily obey Jesus: pray, read scripture
To become His disciple-disciple maker!

Heal our land, today, dear God, heal our land, we pray!
We pray for Your help today to be Your witness!

- **F** — Faith to Believe in Jesus always;
- **O** — Obedience to Follow Jesus;
- **R** — Repentance to Receive Salvation;
- **C** — Compassion to Love and Pray for all;
- **E** — Emmanuel, "God With Us" to Trust;
- **F** — Fullness of Life, with great Joy, receive;
- **U** — Unfailing Abiding in God's Word;
- **L** — Living God's Call and divine Purpose.

"But you will receive power when the Holy Spirit comes on you; and you will be my witnesses in Jerusalem, and in all Judea and Samaria , and to the ends of the earth" (Acts 1:8).

"If my people, who are called by my name, will humble themselves and pray, and seek my face and turn from their wicked ways, then I will hear from heaven, and I will forgive their sin and will heal their land" (2 Chronicles 7:14).

In Your Presence

Because You live,
>	I can be fearless to face tomorrow;

Because You live,
>	I can confidently draw near to You;

Because You live,
>	I now can reject guilt, shame and sorrow;

Because You live,
>	I now have peace that's permanent and true;

In Your Presence,
>	I'm transformed and made wonderfully whole;

In Your Presence,
>	t'is now well with my heart, my mind, and my soul!

Inspiration for this poem came from the devotional *Because He Lives*, written by Nancy (Warwick) Kingdon and available as a download on the author's website, www.writinglegacy.com.

Life's Greatest Question

Life's greatest question is not: "How long did you live?"
No, life's greatest question: "How much joy did you give?"
Before you have blessings to pour out to others,
You must first receive God's love, empowered to serve,
Overflowing, in fact, gifting sisters, brothers
With words of hope, salt-shakers able to preserve.

Wedding of the Lamb

Imagine angel choirs teaching us:
"Of all the seventy names for Jesus,
He chose just one name for His wedding day.
He chose "Lamb" for His love song serenade;
All eyes aren't on the bride, but on the groom!"

All rejoicing hearts turn towards Jesus,
Who rescued His bride, redeemed her, saved her,
And promised to love her forevermore;
Thanksgiving overwhelms heart of the bride,
As the groom embraces His beloved;

Thanksgiving fills our hearts, knowing His love;
We make ourselves ready to meet our God!
Let us rejoice and be glad and give him
Glory! For the wedding of the Lamb has
Come and his bride has made herself ready.

Inspiration for this poem came from an insight offered during Bible study in 2023 on the book of Revelation, taught by Rev. Rick Busse, lead pastor at Evangel Pentecostal Church in Oshawa, Ontario. He highlighted the importance of Jesus choosing to call Himself "the Lamb" instead of any of His other seventy names He could have chosen. Therefore, His loving gift of Himself, and His sacrifice for humanity's sins is what Jesus wants His bride, the Church, to treasure most! See Revelation 17:7.

Wisdom's Path

Wisdom's ways are pleasant ways, and all her paths are peace!
Through wisdom—riches, honour, long life, joy will increase;
Take hold of wisdom, walk in her ways, hold fast to her,
Till blessings beyond measure pursue son and daughter
Like the tree of life, grace canopy shades us from above
As wisdom's peace wraps us close, warming us with God's love!

"*Long life is in her* (wisdom's) *right hand; in her left hand are riches and honor. Her ways are pleasant ways, and all her paths are peace. She is a tree of life to those who take hold of her; those who hold her fast will be blessed*" (Proverbs 3:16–18).

Zesty Fruit of the Spirit

I ask for fruit of the Spirit, dear God,
love, joy, peace given as angels applaud;

patience as forbearance, kindness comes next
teaching Galatians 5, God's goodness text.

goodness, such goodness, given as God's gift,
produces gentleness, grace words that lift

hearts of many, making each one feel blessed,
as self-control completes fruit harvest's zest!

nothing can come against such powerful
transformation—grace-healed hearts now fruitful!

nothing can come against such powerful
righteousness---faith-healed minds now fruitful!

"But the fruit of the Spirit is love, joy, peace, forbearance, kindness, goodness, faithfulness, gentleness and self-control. Against such things there is no law" (Galatians 5:22–23).

"For the kingdom of God is not a matter of eating and drinking, but of righteousness, peace and joy in the Holy Spirit" (Romans 14:17).

Chapter 5

Hope

TABLE OF CONTENTS

Calling on the Name of Lord God Almighty	78
Cathedral Space: A Heart Song of Deep Spiritual Longing	79
Divine Hope	80
Faith Seeds Planted	81
Free from Fear and Anxiety	82
Jesus' Name	83
Joy Path Felt: My Prayer Today for You	84
Light of Truth	85
Lit in God's Sight	86
Mouths Glowing Hope	87
Path of Righteousness (song)	88
Pathways of Peace	89
Prayerful Preserve Jars	90
Reflections on Cities Made Whole	91
Wisdom and Revelation	92

Themes in this chapter nclude hope, peace and wisdom.

Calling on the Name of Lord God Almighty

Hope is ours when we call on Your name
To restore, to revive us, Your face
Shining on us, Your favour given—
That we may be saved, forgiven!

You make known to us the path of life,
In Your Presence You fill us with joy,
Eternal pleasures at your right hand
Flood our lives with inheritance grand!

"*You make known to me the path of life; you will fill me with joy in your presence, with eternal pleasures at your right hand*" (Psalm 16:11).

"*Let your hand rest on the man at your right hand, the son of man you have raised up for yourself. Then we will not turn away from you; revive us, and we will call on your name. Restore us, Lord God Almighty; make your face shine on us, that we may be saved*" (Psalm 80:17–19).

Cathedral Space: A Heart Song of Deep Spiritual Longing

Architects know that space, like clay, is raw material for creative design;
Spiritual leaders know that vintage faith hearts, like wine skins, strengthen over time;

Imagine a heart entering cathedral space, a place of beauty and worship,
Stillness, awe, peace, radiating light, pureness of soul, freedom's lovely fellowship;

Imagine a mind absorbing unfathomable knowledge, glimpses of pure joy,
As flashes of insight, unfolding fireflies, understanding's stars—call like child's toy,

Delighting the soul, healing the heart, inspiring the mind, freeing spirit to soar
On wings of worship, on transformation's breeze, on love song poems that hearts adore;

Listening choirs of angels glorify God, grace's golden nectar from above
Pouring below, through, in, and out of creation, sweet fountains of majestic love,

Belonging's hug, cinnamon toast scents like home, welcoming, lingering, inviting
Holiness, making all things whole, set free, despair gone, hurts mended, minds renewing;

Hope for a better tomorrow, a transformed world, a fresh faith awakening,
Awe's voices set free to declare the glory of God, poetry's streams blossoming!

"God is spirit, and his worshipers must worship in the Spirit and in truth" (John 4:24).

Divine Hope

this kingdom of God
beyond us, and profound,
divine hope our embracing;

yet still touchable,
as God opens our eyes,
our faith now activated;

> revealed
> released
> received

to see the impossible
to touch eternal things
expecting mighty works

> hidden
> miracles
> magnified

> choirs of rejoicing
> harmonizing healed hearts
> astonishing with wonder

> released
> revealed
> received

divine hope, our embracing
beyond us, and profound
this kingdom of God!

Inspiration for this poem came from the words of Oscar Romero: "The kingdom is not only beyond our efforts, it is even beyond our vision. We accomplish in our lifetime only a tiny fraction of the magnificent enterprise that is God's work. Nothing we do is complete, which is a way of saying that the kingdom always lies beyond us."[5]

---

[5] "The Romero Prayer," The Archbishop Romero Trust, accessed December 4, 2024, http://www.romerotrust.org.uk/romero-prayer.

Faith Seeds Planted

Today plant FAITH seeds
To grow a fruitful garden!

F	Faith	**F**	FAITH is believing in God;
A	Amazement	**A**	AMAZEMENT sees miracles;
I	Insight	**I**	INSIGHT comes, reading God's Word;
T	Trust	**T**	TRUST in God builds faithfulness;
H	Hope	**H**	HOPE grows seeds … flourishing faith!

"And without faith it is impossible to please God, because anyone who comes to him must believe that he exists and that he rewards those who earnestly seek him" (Hebrews 11:6).

Free from Fear and Anxiety

We have nothing to fear when You are near, dear God!
Thank You for opening our hearts to hear Your voice
Speaking obedience and truth as Your heart's choice

As we learn to want what You want and do Your will
Your mercy invites us today to surrender
 Our will—battle won against tough, strong contender

In Christ Jesus we pray and ask God for His help;
Praise God we have no anxiety when You're near;
Thank You for peace, guarding our hearts and minds from fear!

"*Do not be anxious about anything, but in every situation, by prayer and petition, with thanksgiving, present your requests to God. And the peace of God, which transcends all understanding, will guard your hearts and your minds in Christ Jesus*" (Philippians 4:6–7).

"*Perfect love drives out fear*" (1 John 4:18).

Jesus' Name

J	Jesus' Name is God's GREAT DIVIDE, the line that separates all;
E	Excellence and restoration for humanity, His call;
S	Severing strongholds of sin, and Satan's hold on everyone,
U	Unifying creation in Jesus' name, new hope begun,
S	Securing hearts through Jesus' cross; it's finished! Battle's won!
'	

N	Name above all names, in heaven and on earth, name supreme!
A	All powerful, able all of humanity to redeem,
M	Manifold wisdom released, beloved restored church's heart,
E	Embraced, rekindled compassion found, as revivals' fires start!

Joy Path Felt: My Prayer Today for You

J	JOY PATH FELT is my prayer for you today,
O	OPENING your heart to feel God's delight,
Y	YEARNING to give you spiritual sight!
P	PEACE, following Jesus' gospel, His way!
A	ARISING joy, knowing God as a friend;
T	TRUST always in God's goodness, through road's bend,
H	HOPE lighting next path, beginning to end!
F	FAITH I pray for you, expanding faith's depth,
E	EMPOWERING wholeness with your next breath,
L	LOVE guiding your footsteps day after day,
T	TRUTH flowing encouragement, joy to stay!

Note: This is my prayer journal entry today on August 9, 2022, for our five children and five grandchildren!

Light of Truth

I believe in Jesus, Saviour and Lord,
I believe Jesus has conquered the grave,
Light of Truth overcomes lies and discord!

In the gospel message, hope I receive;
My eyes are opened; I see with fresh sight
Jesus' favour upon all who believe!

Just as the sun rises each day with light,
Truth penetrates unbelief and deceit,
Till faith in Jesus soars, bringing delight!

Inspiration for this poem came from a quotation by C.S.LEWIS, 1898–1963, "I believe in Christianity as I believe that the sun has risen; I believe not only because I see it but because by it I see everything else."[6]

---

[6] "C.S. Lewis Quotes," Goodreads, accessed November 23, 2024, https://www.goodreads.com/quotes/10209405-i-believe-in-christianity-as-i-believe-that-the-sun.

Lit in God's Sight

LIT IN GOD'S SIGHT!
    I pray for help to SUBMIT my will and my desires today,
        do what is RIGHT,

R	Resting now in righteousness's testing;
I	Inspired to speak, godliness-wired;
G	Grace to pray, radiance on each face;
H	Hope always, rejoicing vision's scope;
T	Trust received, lit in graciousness's thrust.

Mouths Glowing Hope

Deep inside, deep cleansing of minds, hearts, souls
Leads to MOUTHS

    Minds-**O**-**U**-**T**-**H**earts-**S**ouls

    washed clean, able to speak
With GLOWING words of well-being, wholeness, wisdom

    Goodness-**L**ife-**O**neness-**W**ell-being-**W**holeness-**W**isdom-
                               G   L   O   W   **I-N-G**

This GLOWING

    Holiness-**O**neness-**P**eace-**E**mpowerment

HOPE
        shining through godliness's goals, to speak of God's glory!

Path of Righteousness
(song)

I rejoice now in the light of Your love
    and in Your salvation from above
    shining through our lives, radiating hope!
    Hallelujah, Hallelujah, Hallelujah!

I thank You now for opening our ears
    awakening compassionate tears
    and opening our eyes
    to want what You want!
    Hallelujah, Hallelujah, Hallelujah!

May God's will be done today,
    as we choose Your way
    and take righteousness's path
    forward this day, learning how to pray!
    Hallelujah, Hallelujah, Hallelujah!

"The path of the righteous is like the morning sun, shining ever brighter until the full light of day" (Proverbs 4:18).

Pathways of Peace

Come, take peace's pathway today
    Anchor cast, learning how to pray.

Align inner hearts with healing,
    Assign minds with words appealing,

Permeate peace as a pathway
    Peace flourishing, here to stay!

Eyes seeing revelations sharp
    New visions—hope's dreams to impart.

Prayerful Preserve Jars

P	PEACE-MAKERS, combat hurt
E	EVERYDAY on alert
A	ALWAYS Word's salt-shakers
C	CARING and forgiving
E	ENCOURAGING, trusting
S	SHARING food and friendship
H	HEARTS in relationship
E	EMPOWERING truth's sight
L	LOVE flowing with delight
F	FAITH preserving hope's light!

Think of each one of us as preserve jars on a shelf, vessels filled with God's jam, pickles, relishes, and other food, ready to share with others something that is uniquely savoury yet nourishing.

Reflections on Cities Made Whole

Neighbourhoods, streets, parks, and homes
Filled with healed hearts, transformed,
Love-bathed, sparkling with new hope,
Lit identity restored

Hearts made whole by great spaces
Belonging's beckoning hands
Learning's instructions released
Dignity redesigning

How people see, hear, and speak
As together our city
Comes alive with a new voice
Of beauty, roots of deep love

Planted as thoughts are spoken
Prayer-rooted ideas give
People a message to say
Hope emerging to build up

Not tear down, but reconstruct
Neighbourhoods, streets, parks, and homes
Creativity embraced
To know God's AUTHORITY

Imagining cities changed
Reshaped by God's divine love
People sparkling with new voice
Joyful cities arising!

Inspiration for this poem came from "author" imbedded in the word "authority" and the hint of the word "city" found in the same word.

Wisdom and Revelation

God's Word teaches us how to live and pray,
Guiding us forward in a straight path, God's way;

You are invited to ask for wisdom,
Promised wisdom's receipt, plus treasure's sum!

But did you know that you should also ask
For something else, needed for every task?

To grasp God's love for all of creation,
Ask for the Spirit of revelation.

Revelation is needed to know God
Better, able to see how high and broad

And powerful God's love, breaking cages,
Unstoppable power throughout ages;

So high, wide, deep, long love's majestic sweep
God's holy inheritance it can keep!

Our limited minds cannot comprehend
How love conquers condemnation, to mend

Hearts destroyed by sin's abomination
Hurting, maiming minds, contamination

Leaving people feeling hopeless and lost,
Enticed, imprisoned in sin's senseless cost;

Unwilling they are, to fight deceit's decay,
We must ask God for revelation today:

Eyes opening to see His unfailing love,
Flooding lands with hope's rivers from above!

"Where there is no revelation, people cast off restraint; but blessed is the one who heeds wisdom's instruction" (Proverbs 29:18).

"I keep asking that the God of our Lord Jesus Christ, the glorious Father, may give you the Spirit of wisdom and revelation, so that you may know him better" (Ephesians 1:17).

"'For my thoughts are not your thoughts, neither are your ways my ways,' declares the Lord. 'As the heavens are higher than the earth, so are my ways higher than your ways and my thoughts than your thoughts'" (Isaiah 55:8–9).

Chapter 6
Restoration

TABLE OF CONTENTS

Breathing in and Out	96
Building a Dwelling Place	97
Celebrating Sparkling Snow Bees	98
Chapel Songs	100
Deliver Us Today, I Pray!	101
Erasing Sin Through Grace	102
Hearts Holding Holiness	103
Hearts Set Free	104
Light Shines Through	105
One Single Moment	106
Paths of Peace	107
Polished Beach Glass Hearts	108
Shake Up Our World Through Servanthood Attitudes!	109
To Love and Be Loved	110
Truth Wrestles Lies to the Ground	111

Themes in this chapter include restoration, healing, and deliverance.

Breathing in and Out

I breathe in Jesus, pure, clean hope I inhale,
    in, in, in I breathe in hope;
  I breathe out darkness, hangman's rope I exhale,
    out, out, out I cut sin's rope;
I breathe in Jesus, His Presence, I inhale,
    in, in, in I breathe in faith;
  I breathe out apathy's doubt, doubt I exhale,
    out, out, out I break doubt's choke;
I breathe in Jesus, His living Word I inhale,
    in, in, in I breathe in truth;
  I breathe out deception, distrust I exhale,
    out, out, out I snap distrust's scope.

Building a Dwelling Place

When God is our dwelling place, doors open;
First, within us as our hearts are healed;
Secondly, with new opportunities;
Thirdly, as hearts respond to God's purpose
At work through our choice to follow Jesus,
And we are able to love and obey
God, joining Him in movements He has planned.

When we are God's dwelling place, things happen
Beyond our capacity and limits;
God's Spirit walks, talks, and guides us forward
To want what God wants for us and others,
To do what we can only do through God,
Equipping us for impacting the world
For good, and to make it a better place.

Is your dwelling place inside or outside
The heart of God and His divine purpose—
To bless you and make you His great blessing
To your family, friends, neighbours, city?
Have you invited God to dwell in you,
Making your heart His renovation plan,
To build a new magnificent dwelling?

While reading Revelation 17 and 21, I caught awareness that Babylon, the Prostitute, was a city controlled by Satan and Jerusalem, yet the Bride is a city controlled by God. While we are asked to make God our trustworthy dwelling place, we are also encouraged to invite Jesus to make our hearts His dwelling place, so that He can transform us from what we were to what He wants us to become!

Celebrating Sparkling Snow Bees

Once upon a time, in the land of rhyme,
Where time stops stretching forward as straight line,
I remember a cross-country trail bend
Opening into a wonderland blend
Of branches wearing icicle rings round,
Falling snowflakes fluttering, nearing ground;

I felt like I was in an awesome place—
Otherworldly, outside earth and known space;
That's when it happened—my heart drummed fast
My eyes gazed, my mouth dropped—aghast!
Sparkling white lights danced on a tall tree,
Like snow bees they twirled and whirled free.

Why this image seared itself in my soul,
I don't know, but it did, making me heal—
In a way that shocked me, causing wet tears
To sear my heart, evaporating fears,
Replacing former scars with joy's increase
As each light told a story of release!

In that moment, time as I knew it stopped;
A spiritual dimension was caught—
That told me each one of us has purpose;
Seek deeper truth, it's not on the surface!
But starting place is to search for wonder,
Like mesmerizing lights, without number.

Dancing delight, with a story to tell
Of release from captivity, a well
Hiding what matters, living Words of Light
Ready to be polished as gems, with might
To speak, to write, to share what God has done
Hope transforming hearts—lights they have become!

Each one of us who knows Jesus as Lord
Has been given God's Word as a TRUTH SWORD
To cut away deceit, to conquer sin,
To fight alongside God, His battles win;
Stand firm—expect miracles to increase,
Radiate Snow Bee joy, healing's release!

Inspiration for this poem came from my personal experience of cross-country skiing and discovering a cloud of sparkling white lights hovering over a tree, like dancing snow bees, I thought. This image has been retained, exciting my imagination since 1985. I hope it captures your thoughts with as much wonder and beauty as I have enjoyed for over three decades.

Chapel Songs

C	comfort	C	creativity
H	hope	H	healing
A	arising faith	A	amazing joy
P	prayers	P	peace
E	encouragement	E	empowerment
L	love	L	loveliness

chapel songs
of worship
righting all wrongs
to see
promises of God
released,
so free
barriers—decreased

Deliver Us Today, I Pray!

I ask for a new day.
I ask for a new way to pray
I ask for revelation—fresh light's ray
Shining in deliverance, peace to stay
In hearts, till we see all strongholds fade away!
Thank You, dear God, for deliverance, received TODAY!

"*You are my hiding place; you will protect me from trouble and surround me with songs of deliverance*" (Psalm 32: 7).

Erasing Sin Through Grace

    GOD'S WORD
    grace race is
    r
    always
    c
    e
    Word's sword
    ERASING SIN

Grace race's Word swords always erase
sin—holding guilt in—shame's stronghold place;

strength surrounds God's Word, opening gates,
till grace's erasing decreases sin's weights.

love's smile paints faces, with Word reaching
hearts in need of healing and teaching.

Hearts Holding Holiness

H	Hearts holding holiness are transformed
E	Empowered to arise, grace adorned;
A	Awakening to truth, set free from fraud,
R	Repentance first step toward pleasing God;
T	Trusting God a choice—lit identity
S	Seeking God—new daily passionate plea.
H	Holding holiness, hearts are reformed,
O	Obedience to God's Word implored;
L	Loving kindness seen, heard, revealed, a norm,
D	Delivered from sin—broken strongholds torn;
I	Illumination pushing back darkness, creating path's light
N	Nearing God, hearts holding holiness bright,
G	Godliness, God's gracious gift of delight!
H	Holiness held in hearts reveals God's grace,
O	Obedience bringing smiles on each face;
L	Loving kindness seen, heard, revealed, a norm,
I	Intentionality plowing through storm,
N	Nearing God, empowered to win each fight;
E	Empowerment to discern wrong from right,
S	Sanctification received, hearts healed,
S	Satisfaction filling hearts, love revealed!

Hearts Set Free

Lord, please bind up Satan near us,
Guide us—by Your Spirit, steer us!

H	Help us listen and guard our ears;
E	Expand peace, wipe away our tears,
A	Align all hearts, expanding years;
R	Release Your love, removing fears,
T	Today, excite rejoicing's cheers;
S	Satisfied, give grace that endears!

Thank You for freeing us today,
Thank You for teaching us to pray.

Light Shines Through

LIGHT
SHINES
T-H-R-O-U-G-H

penetrates the darkness, cutting

T-H-R-O-U-G-H

With	Words	with	Works
With	Oneness	with	Obedience
With	Righteousness	with	Repentance
With	Dawn's Dew	with	Deliverance
With	Salvation	with	Sanctification

One Single Moment

Life sometimes rests on a single moment;
Did you know that Jesus' ministry stay
Was recorded as three and a half years?
That's only twenty-nine days, less one day,
Of Jesus' life noted in God's Word.

Shrinking time into a bottle like this,
And tossing testimonies out to sea,
Bring miracles—like healing stories' bliss,
Making hearts sing with excitement, fancy free,
Because we have power in one moment!

In one encounter with a single heart,
Short blink of an eye, as Truth's Word is sent
To impact someone searching for God' love!
One Word planted in good soil can prevent
Heartache, can spark healing, transformation!

Changing life's direction, from sin's recoil;
Dramatic about-turn toward God's hand.
All that matters, funneled into a choice,
Time's framed moment, righteous choice's upright stand
Eclipsing years, sparking decision's voice!

To believe in Jesus, following Him!
To turn away from deceit, seeking Truth,
Aware that each hope-anointed breath counts,
To someone, somewhere—answered prayers our proof!
That life can rest on a single moment!

Inspiration for this poem came from Isaiah 37:21. Because they prayed, God moved to resolve a problem and victory was given.

Paths of Peace

Have you ever pondered the way
God's gifts of GRACE, MERCY, POWER
Can conjure GLIMPSES of insight?
Thoughts, ideas, words you can pray?

Have you ever pondered the way
God's gifts of POWER, MERCY, GRACE
Can cause PILGRIMAGING journeys
Thoughts, ideas, words you can pray?

Have you ever pondered the way
God's gifts of MERCY, POWER, GRACE
Can complete MAPPING strategies
Thoughts, ideas, words you can pray?

Glimpses of truth give divine revelations and dreams;
Pilgrimages touch hem of Jesus' garment, stitched seams
Bringing healing, deliverance, and opening path
To pray for healing of nations—God's mercy, not wrath!

Polished Beach Glass Hearts

To heal, let go of past, take hold of hope—
Now, move forward with purpose, vision's scope,
To be made whole, great spaces revealing,
Recovering from rejection's feeling,
Shattered shards of broken glass edges hurt,
Wounding like sputtering sound's final spurt.

Whispering wisps of words float by, intriguing ear,
Reminding us to focus, listen, and to hear
What nature would teach us, as puffs of winds soar past
Then return, circling back, swirling, whirling so fast
Their voice hovers with thoughts that need to be snatched,
Like strings of melodies, sporadic and patched.

We see foaming white spray pushing sand from the sea
Out, out away from the shore, way past depth of knee,
There to rest awhile before journeying onwards,
Searching for old broken bottles, shattered piece shards,
Now polished beach glass beauty, ready to astound
Finger's touch with soft smooth surface, smooth stones made round.

How awesome when hearts are healed, set free, transformed
Blessed, made whole by sand's grace, forgiven, polished
With whispering words, hope and truth made powerful
To heal brokenness, even cleansing inside skull,
Ending distorted thoughts, deaf ears, myopic eyes,
Till hearts, like radiant beach glass, with joy arise!

Inspiration for this poem came from Lorna Tatomir's draft manuscript (soon to be published), tentatively titled *Beach Glass Women*.

Shake Up Our World Through Servanthood Attitudes!

Today, let's grow your business,
Business barriers hurled!
SHAKE UP your daily habits
with servanthood attitudes!

S	Serving. Want to feel good about yourself?
H	Happiness. Want to attract customers?
A	Appreciation. Want happy people?
K	Kindness. Want to expand your leadership?
E	Enthusiasm. Want new investors?
U	Understanding. Want your voice to be heard?
P	Patience. Give it if you want to receive patience.
S	Serving others is good soul medicine! Value everyone.
H	Happiness is contagious! Build a caring, smiling, great team.
A	Appreciation warms hearts! Daily be thankful toward all.
K	Kindness touches hearts. Build places where belonging flourishes.
E	Enthusiasm is contagious! Build trust relationships.
U	Understanding grows through listening ears! Listen more; talk less.
P	Patience is a virtue! Stop taking offense; stop complaining.

Note: Where the word "servanthood" is used, you can also substitute "ministry," or even "business," "volunteerism," or "life"!

To Love and Be Loved

when someone knows
that one is loved by another heart,
sincerely;

when someone knows
that one can love another heart back,
sincerely;

surely that is
the most valuable
lesson that anyone needs to learn!

surely that is
the most valuable
life purpose: to love and to be loved!

"*Jesus replied: 'Love the Lord your God with all your heart and with all your soul and with all your mind, This is the first and greatest commandment. And the second is like it: Love your neighbour as yourself'*" (Matthew 22:37–39).

Truth Wrestles Lies to the Ground

In prayer I caught hold of the fact that God
Hurts when His children hurt—tangled and torn
In bondages, in rejection's sharp claws,
That cause reactions, strong triggers, to lies;
Activating hurts again and again,
Sometimes for years, decades repetitive
Reactions to something, based on a lie;
Yet truth's deliverance is possible!

And prayer can ignite God's warpath response,
To fight the source of the pain, the big lie—
That horrible feeling of rejection
That destroys lives, slashes belonging's roots,
And ignites hostile reaction, not love,
As response, reinforcing the big lie!
Today, let's ask God for His truth to cut
Through the big lie of rejection's stronghold!

When God's heart breaks with yearning for His child,
May God's wisdom and revelation come!
His anointing truth and hope now become
Our deliverance song from the big lie—loud
Our rejoicing—hearts set free, lifted high, proud
To know how deeply God cares and delights
In healing loved ones, through truth's light and joy
As truth activates belonging's heart cries!

May God's truth today devour rejection;
May God's truth today release belonging.
Truth wrestles lies to the ground, all around
Silencing barbed-wire bites, negating blights,
Till love has a chance to breathe fresh air in,
Embracing new hope, hugging holiness;
God's Word of truth's our antidote to fright,
Breaking the bondage of rejection's hurt!

Chapter 7
Oneness

TABLE OF CONTENTS

Church Contemplations: Unity	114
Creative Vowels	115
Empowerment	116
Grow in Power	117
Hope's Oneness of Heart	118
Hope's Radiance	120
Igniting Lit Identity Through Pondering Name of Jesus	121
Infinite Love	122
Intimacy with God	123
Majestic Melodies in Motion	124
Oneness Arising	125
Oneness's Waves	126
Proof Requested	127
Rooms to Explore	128
Uniting All	129

Themes in this chapter include oneness, unity, and mercy.

Church Contemplations: Unity

C   Core value is Jesus Christ as our leader
H   Hope
U   Unity, through oneness of heart
R   Rejoicing
C   Compassion
H   Happiness is found in Christ Jesus alone

Creative Vowels

Prayerful love songs of A E I O U
filling our land with fresh understanding
of God's majestic plan for me and you

I thank God for **e**ndless love **u**nfailing,
For **o**neness love, alive, alive, alive
 for **a**bundant **i**nfinite love, unending,

unforgettable a e i o u
unstoppable valiant voice alive
victorious plan for me and for you!

To speak, to write, to tell God's love story
His Story alive in me and in you,
Our voices sharing God's grace-filled glory

Empowerment

Pray for a move of God, empowered;
Pray for hearts and minds now opened;
Pray for God's Purposes to guide us!

E	empowerment
M	mercy
P	provision
O	oneness
W	wisdom
E	expansion
R	revelation
M	movement
E	encouragement
N	nourishment
T	trust

Praise the Lord for empowerment's dance;
Praise the Lord for God's strength to advance!
Praise the Lord for His Holy Spirit's help!

"*Where there is no revelation, people cast off restraint; but blessed is the one who heeds wisdom's instruction*" (Proverbs 29:18).

"*I keep asking that the God of our Lord Jesus Christ, the glorious Father, may give you the Spirit of wisdom and revelation, so that you may know him better*" (Ephesians 1:17).

Grow in Power

Come, Holy Spirit!

- **G**   Gracious God, above
- **R**   Release Your divine Purpose, Come, Holy Spirit in Power;
- **O**   Oneness heart of love
- **W**   Wrap us in Your Presence, Your Love, and fill us this day, this hour

in

- **P**   Power, shifts the atmosphere;
- **O**   Oneness opens eyes to see;
- **W**   Wisdom helps us to hear God;
- **E**   Empowerment gives us strength;
- **R**   Repentance realigns heart's purpose.

Hope's Oneness of Heart

Whoever seeks God will find hope, His hidden identity;
Hope reflects radiance of God's essence, His nature to be
All that humanity needs and desires,
All that His family feels and admires,
When God's desires match our prayers and heart's search
House of Prayer'll be His new call for His church!
celebrating Oneness of heart, at last
Hope flooding present, future, and the past!

H	O	U	S	E
e	n	n	a	m
a	e	d	t	p
l	n	e	i	o
i	e	r	s	w
n	s	s	f	e
g	s	t	y	r
		a	i	e
		n	n	d
		d	g	
		i		
		n		
		g		

OF

P	R	A	Y	E	R
r	e	w	e	x	e
a	j	a	a	c	v
i	o	k	r	I	e
s	I	e	n	t	l
i	c	n	i	i	a
n	i	i	n	n	t
g	n	n	g	g	i
	g	g			o
					n

What a star of hope is God's **HOUSE OF PRAYER**
His Oneness of Heart Church empowered to care!

Hope's Radiance

What radiance God's **HOPE OF SALVATION** offers!
What satisfaction God's **WORD OF LIFE** offers!

H	Healing
O	Overcoming
P	Purposelessness
E	Emptiness
'	
S	Satisfied in God's Presence
W	Wisdom
O	Oneness
R	Revelation
D	Discernment
O	Opens minds to understand
F	Faith's purposes and promises
L	Love's
I	Inspirational
F	Fullness and
E	Empowerment

Igniting Lit Identity Through Pondering Name of Jesus

May we walk today in the glorious name of Jesus,
Most majestic, merciful, magnificent, marvellous
Name ever breathed, spoken, revealed;
His Unfolding Oneness
Immersed in Holiness,
Reflecting unfailing Goodness!

So strong, so powerful, so mighty, every knee must bow
Before His beloved name, Jesus' heart made known, somehow
His character shining through Scripture, God's Word captured—caught—
Proclaiming something hidden, something deeper than our thought!
Yet once revealed, capable of transforming every heart,
Illuminating challenges, wisdom's voice to impart
A pathway of righteousness, inviting us forward, forward,
Away from crowds, media, thought patterns gazing backward,

Eyes focused, feet walking, calling out the name of Jesus;
Most majestic, merciful, magnificent, marvellous
Name ever breathed, spoken,
Hands reaching in unity,
Immersed in rejoicing, Igniting Lit Identity!

Infinite Love

      Who is God? God is infinite LOVE!
W   Wonder awakens hearts to listen—
      When LOVE speaks, joy's tears in hearts glisten!

      Hearing, seeing, knowing Who GOD is,
H   Heals our brokenness, breaks sins' stronghold;
      Holiness rekindling voices bold.

      Oneness our destiny through Jesus,
O   Obedience is our deep desire,
      Opening minds, passions set on fire!

"God is love. Whoever lives in love lives in God, and God in them" (1 John 4:16).

"Dear friends, let us love one another, for love comes from God. Everyone who loves has been born of God and knows God. Whoever does not love does not know God, because God is love" (1 John 4:7–8).

Intimacy with God

L	Lost in Holy Spirit's Presence, staying
I	Inside, inside the heart of God!
Q	Quiet time alone with Jesus, praying
U	Under, under counsel of God!
I	Immersed in God's Presence, alive in light,
D	Daring to listen, faith's eyes growing sight.
L	Love received, heart opening like flower,
O	Opening, opening to peace;
V	Voice of God heard, activating power,
E	Empowering release, release.
P	Power given, understanding renewed,
O	Over, over the work of God
U	Understanding's hour of wisdom pursued,
R	Releasing miracles of God;
I	Immersed in God's Presence, alive in might,
N	Now mercy flowing, unfurling what's right,
G	Growing gardens of pure delight!
O	Oneness of vision, unfolding great dreams,
U	Uniting, uniting all hearts,
T	Treasuring Jesus, who redeems!
I	Intimacy with God—peace's measure found;
N	Nothing, nothing satisfies more!
T	Trustworthiness deep, seeds planted in ground,
I	Inside brokenness, blood will pour
M	Mercy, like liquid love bubbling hope;
A	Amazing lifeline, belonging's strong rope
C	Carries me safely through illness, weakness,
Y	Yearning's intimacy deepens stillness.

Majestic Melodies in Motion

prayers and love released, set free, flowing, fullness of God's heart filling all of creation,
magnified majestic melodies of mercy flood our land with God's healing power,
up, down, in, out, through, forward, backward, upside down, right side up,
stitching, glueing, papering, painting, sanding, varnishing, stapling,
cutting, sculpting, shaping
transforming
redesigning
renovating
remaking
restoring
redoing
uniting
healing
mercy;
hearts
made
new
oneness's
majestic
melodies
in motion

Oneness Arising

ONENESS, like fresh ink on hand-crafted paper, like divine swirls of thoughts
      O---Pen hearts   O---Pen minds   O---Pen souls
to something felt, known, experienced but unable to be described
through words;
to something illusive, deposited deep within the soul,
like a hidden dormant song,
awaiting a touch,
a spark of ONENESS releasing threads of vibrations,
forming,
a pattern of poetic pondering on a page, like fresh ink on hand-crafted paper,
like divine swirls of thoughts, musical notes,
forming,
woven wonder, dots on linen vellum, scripted music beautiful as invisible
prayers,
felt, known, experienced deep inside, awakening soul's inner landscape to
praise,
empowering new beginnings, a new day's dawn.
ONENESS arising as uninhibited
power!

Oneness's Waves

w   w   w
world wide web   turning away
                              activating
                              knowledge
                              embracing
wisdom   as   voice   empowered
w   a   v   e
                              after wave
                              rushing faith
                              toward
drowning pockets of hidden darkness,
where some wander, lost in holes of tangled hopelessness;

each wave empowered to take art forward,
each wave empowered to take faith forward,
wisdom's voice like a wave, circling, searching crescendo,
inviting hearts to grasp lifeline, preserve hope, hold on tight!

Proof Requested

Please heal our land, dear Lord, heal Canada!
After a prayer time with the Lord today,
I heard Your inspiring Spirit's voice say:
PROOF is what I ask, that I am in charge!
PROOF I ask because my mercy's so large!

Please heal our land, dear Lord, heal Canada!
Please heal our First Nations peoples, Your way!
For Ontario and Oshawa, delay
Punishment for evil, what's so deserved,
Giving instead mercy, Your grace reserved!

P	PRAYERS PROPHECY POETRY PROMISES PRAISES					**P**
R	REJOICING					**R**
O	ONENESS					**O**
O	ONENESS					**O**
F	FRAGRANCE FREEDOM FULLNESS FAVOUR FAITH					**F**

Note for pondering: MERCY is given when God withholds punishment that our sins deserve, and GRACE is given when God gives us unmerited goodness.

Rooms to Explore

God's heart has rooms to enter and explore;
I see kitchen table, polished wood floor,
Rich mahogany tones, cupboards gleam white,
And I long to sit here, sharing a meal,
Listening to His voice, nothing to conceal,
Basking in His Presence, our faces bright.

Down the hall, I enter a library,
Books everywhere, life's memoirs some carry;
Ladders, carved from oak, line entire wall,
They reach upper shelves, ten-foot-high ceilings,
Holding hope's words, encouragement's healings,
Making me feel like reading, wrapped in wool shawl.

Outside I see a gazebo garden,
Yellow gladiolas, petals open,
Cushions soft on deck chairs, gas-fire nearby,
Beckoning me into oasis space;
So comfortable, relaxation's pace,
Like honey, as songbirds fly by in sky.

It's an adventure to walk through God's heart,
Seeking to know Him—listening ears start
Seeing anew, eyes gazing in wonder—
Perfectly balanced, everything's just right,
Nothing's out of place, just pleasing insight
In God's Presence, as dawn's songs you'll ponder!

"*But I, by your great love, can come into your house; in reverence I bow down toward your holy temple*" (Psalm 5:12).

"*Surely, Lord, you bless the righteous; you surround them with your favor as with a shield*" (Psalm 5:7).

Uniting All

"From Him all things, and to Him all things,"
Voices sang, closing with explosive words,
Full of praise, "You deserve the glory!"
As Alpha and Omega, God reigns,
Connecting Beginning and Ending,
Uniting, through love, all of creation!

"I have given them the glory that you gave me, that they may be one as we are one—I in them and you in me—so that they may be brought to complete unity. Then the world will know that you sent me and have loved them even as you have loved me" (John 17:22–23).

Chapter 8
Obedience

TABLE OF CONTENTS

Answering God's Call	132
Building Capacity in Canada: Part 1	133
Building Capacity in Canada: Part 2	134
Call to Repentance	135
Credit Account	136
Disciple's Prayer	137
Do You Love Me?	138
Eight Characteristics of Christlikeness	139
Eternity's Choice	141
Jars of Clay	143
Mentors Impact the Next Generation	144
Mobilizing a Mentoring Movement	145
Radar, Rodney's Bear	146
Servant Leadership	147
Virtues to Value	148
Yoked with You	149

Themes in this chapter include obedience, discipleship, path, and mentoring.

Answering God's Call

Each one of us has a calling, a task
We are asked by God to do, to serve Him,
Not to get anything, but to give thanks
For His gift of forgiveness, conquering sin!

Do you have a book to write, a legacy story to tell,
That fills your heart with longing, and passion?
Do you have a calling to write a prayer, a message of hope,
That you know will touch hearts with compassion?

Don't delay! Don't put it off to cause guilt!
Answer the call, accept God's commission!
Start today! Write your story, your memoirs,
Or do something for God, as your mission!

One day you will want to hear God's voice speak:
"Well done, my good and faithful servant! Come!"
Enter the kingdom of Your Lord and God;
"Good job! It is finished! Your work is done!"

Each one of us has a task to do, grace blessings given,
That we must share with others, give or write!
Your life can cause many to turn to God, rejoicing in hope,
Ready to know God better and find sight!

Perhaps you are called to serve in your church,
Teaching ESL, youth, or Sunday School;
You've been given gifts, spiritual gifts
To advance God's kingdom, chosen as God's tool!

Building Capacity in Canada
Part 1

Today, dear friend, let's transform our precious country,
Birthing fresh CAP-A-CITY to see nation healed!
> Pray for Canada to repent, turn from evil;
> Pray for Canada's turn toward God, not away;
> Pray for all Canadians to want what God wants;
> Pray for our leaders to do what's right in God's sight—
> Empowered to shine bright as Lit Identity,
> Touching each church, college, city, community
> Until each one is filled to capacity,
> Unified in serving God, shining with Oneness Heart,
> Ready to radiate God's purposes and love!

Pray for Canada to build fresh love capacity …
New CAP-A-CITY to love, trust God and shine with truth!

Building Capacity in Canada
Part 2

Today, dear friend, let's choose to transform our precious country,
Birthing fresh CAP-A-CITY to see our nation healed!
    I pray for Canada to repent, turn from evil;
    I pray for Canada's turn toward God, not away;
    I pray for all Canadians to want what God wants;
    I pray for our leaders to do what's right in God's sight—
    Now empowered to shine bright as Lit Identity,
    Voices touching church, college, city, community
    Until all are filled to capacity, filled
    Unified in serving God, shining with Oneness Heart,
    Ready now to radiate God's purposes and love!
I pray for Canada to build love capacity …
Fresh CAP-A-CITY to love, trust God and shine with truth!

Note: When reading this poem a second time, substitute "I pray" with "we pray."

Call to Repentance

Repentance is something Jesus calls us to do;
It means turning away from sins that control us;
It means turning toward God choosing pathway new!
Set feet on path north—truth and righteousness's compass

As we target salvation as our greatest need;
Know that we are all sinners, lost sinners indeed!
Ask God for a changed heart, so we can forgive
Those around us, and ourselves, choosing now to live.

In obedience to the call of God to pray,
Seeking to know justice and mercy today.
"Repent, Repent!" we hear Jesus' loud voice instruct,
Salvation has come—as His miracles erupt!

"*On hearing this, Jesus said to them, 'It is not the healthy who need a doctor, but the sick. I have not come to call the righteous, but sinners'*" (Mark 2:17).

"*for all have sinned and fall short of the glory of God*" (Romans 3:23).

"*He has shown you, O mortal, what is good. And what does the Lord require of you? To act justly and to love mercy and to walk humbly with your God*" (Micah 6:8).

Credit Account

Please CREDIT us this day, by Your Spirit
- **C**   Call us
- **R**   Release us
- **E**   Equip us
- **D**   Deliver us
- **I**   Inspire us
- **T**   Teach us

Fill us with Your DESIRES, to do Your will!

Disciple's Prayer

Disciples who want to be disciple-makers
Will pray as Jesus taught His disciples to pray:

Our Father in heaven, hallowed be Your name,
Your kingdom come; Your will be done on earth today,
As it is in heaven. Give us our daily bread;
And forgive us our debts as we have forgiven
Our debtors, and lead us not into temptation,
But deliver us today from the evil one.

Forgiving others must be our lifelong story;
God's kingdom and power is to be our glory!

See Mathew 6:5–15.

Do You Love Me?

When Jesus asks Peter: "Do you love me?"
And he answers three times to Jesus: "Yes!"
What else does Jesus tell Peter to do?
"Feed my lambs," "Care for my sheep," He instructs;
Then He adds: "Feed my sheep" and "Follow me!"

While sheep chew grass, digesting solid food,
Lambs drink milk, staying close to their mother;
While sheep know and follow their shepherd's voice,
Lambs know their mother's voice, following her;
When we love Jesus, our faith must mature!

Faith's newcomers follow other Christians,
Therefore, modeling right and wrong matters!
Caring for others with compassion's heart
Reflects the heart of God in today's world.
Teaching God's Word reveals maturity.

Following Jesus requires discipline,
Obedience, and even suffering;
To feed faith's lambs and to care for God's sheep
Means we must eat, digest God's Word daily,
Then share insights through our speech plus actions.

See John 21:15–22. Inspiration for this poem came from a sermon preached at Evangel Church, Oshawa, Ontario in January 2024.

Eight Characteristics of Christlikeness

Love for God and others is commanded,
And, in fact, is GREATEST command of all!
It can be cultivated through prayer,
Studying scriptures, and acts of kindness;
Unconditional love shines God's goodness!

Humility is what Jesus modelled,
Which means disciples must depend on God
And seek to serve others, as Jesus did;
Having a teachable spirit, wanting
To glorify God, not elevate self.

Obedience to God's Word reflects faith
And shows our love for God's will and His way;
Study the Bible to divide the truth
Accurately, living by its counsel;
Choose accountability partnerships.

Disciplined Prayer and Godly Practices
Abiding in truth and living in Christ
Through fasting, meditation, and prayer
Help build a strong connection with Jesus,
And strengthen spiritual discernment.

As **Disciples and Disciple-Makers,**
Commitment grows, God's kingdom advances,
And each person's mentorship and mission
Will help to equip others to serve God,
Investing in the lives of multitudes!

Generosity and Stewardship will
Prioritize God's purposes on earth,
As in heaven, highlighting Who owns all,
Our belongings, resources, and talents
So God's purposes can benefit all.

Perseverance and Reliance matter
Because God is Sovereign and asks us
To persevere through trials with faith and trust;
God's promises are victoriously
Revealed when we overcome trials through faith.

Spirit-Empowered Living is vital
For a disciple seeking to follow
God's will, guided by the Holy Spirit;
When prayer, worship and listening cause
Surrender, fruit of the Spirit will grow!

See Mathew 22:37–39.

Inspiration for this poem came from Rev. Rich Janes' contribution to *We the Called. Mobilizing a Mentoring Movement*.[7]

---

[7] Rich Janes in *We the Called. Mobilizing a Mentoring Movement*, David Wells and Rich Janes, Eds. (Mississauga, ON: The Pentecostal Assemblies of Canada, 2024), 101–106.

Eternity's Choice

If you have breath, there's still time
To repent, turn toward God,
Invite God to change your heart.

We each have a choice to make:
To obey and follow God,
Or to turn away from love;

Separated from God's love,
For endless eternity,
Rejected, cold and alone.

Mortal, all people will die …
Endless life or endless death
Will be ours forevermore.

Life's biggest question is not:
"Is there life after death?" or
"Does a loving God exist?"

No, life's great question is:
"Do I believe in God's love?"
"Will I choose to embrace God?"

Inspiration for this poem came from reading the introduction to C.S. Lewis's book *The Seeing Eye*, where we learn from Walter Hooper that the central premise of all of Lewis's theological works is that "all men are immortal."[8]

---

[8] C.S. Lewis, *The Seeing Eye* (New York, NY: Ballantine Books, 1967), viii.

"What do workers gain from their toil? I have seen the burden God has laid on the human race. He has made everything beautiful in its time. He has also set eternity in the human heart; yet, no one can fathom what God has done from beginning to end" (Ecclesiastes 3:9–11).

"For God so loved the world that he gave his one and only Son, that whoever believes in him shall not perish but have eternal life" (John 3:16).

"Whoever believes in the Son has eternal life, but whoever rejects the Son will not see life, for God's wrath remains on them" (John 3:36).

Jars of Clay

Justice And Righteousness Strengthen

J   A   R   S   of clay
As God reshapes us into His image today.
The Lord will be exalted by His justice tracks;
God will be proved holy by His righteousness acts.
When God's people obey, doing what's right and good,
God's heart lifts, watching His people living as they should;
When God's people give justice to the poor and oppressed,
Compassion given, they pass love character's test!

"But the Lord Almighty will be exalted by his justice, and the holy God will be proved holy by his righteous acts" (Isaiah 5:16).

Mentors Impact the Next Generation

How passionate are you about discipleship
And planting seeds of truth into young people's minds?
Jesus teaches us that we are called and equipped
To become disciples and disciple-makers,
Vessels holding His truth, designed as saltshakers.

Each one of us is called to impact the world;
One heart at a time, our lives can show Jesus' love,
As we learn to please God and obey His calling,
Using our spiritual gifts to teach and pray
For others, mentoring one another today.

Everyone is called to serve God and to mentor
Others, choosing to commit to nurturing faith,
Seeking to know God and draw closer to God's heart
With humility, obedience, compassion,
So we fulfill God's purpose, serving with passion!

Inspiration for this poem came from reading *We the Called. Mobilizing a Mentoring Movement.* See Mathew 22:37–39.

Mobilizing a Mentoring Movement

Mobilizing a Mentoring Movement
Is the theme of *We the Called*, a book
Produced by PAOC leadership.

Constellation model for mentoring
Builds relationships in three directions:
Upward, downward, and horizontally;

Upward mentoring involves someone with
Less experience seeking a seasoned
Mentor, able to advise and support;

Downward mentoring involves someone with
More experience investing knowledge
To nurture a mentee toward a goal.

Horizontal mentoring results in
Same-level peer group collaboration,
Creating a supportive peer network.

Inspiration for this poem came from *We the Called: Mobilizing a Mentoring Movement* (p.16), where Robert Clinton and Paul Stanley's book, *Connecting: The Mentoring Relationship You Need to Succeed*, is acknowledged as the source for the Constellation Model of Mentorship.

Radar, Rodney's Bear

Rodney's Radar, a friend from his childhood,
Sits on our guest bed, a remnant of love
That began decades ago and withstood
Our five grandchildren and son's baseball glove,
Clutched next to Radar at nightly bedtime,
As daughters too listened to story-time;

How many family memories here;
Even now, tattered Radar's warmth is strong—
Cuddly bear's touch, like a close friend so dear,
Memories treasured, as hearts sing love song;
Opa-Grandma's wedding story—bride-groom
Framed, as grandson Gavin sleeps in guest room.

Inspiration: Our eleven-year-old grandson Gavin slept over in our guest room last night, November 19, 2023, and was told the story of Radar, his Opa's treasured childhood teddy bear.

Servant Leadership

it takes courage to do what's right,
what's right not in our view, but in God's sight.

it takes courage to obey God,
not following the world's loud voice of fraud.

generosity takes intentional action,
passionate love's response without sin's reaction.

be courageous now and bold, take action today;
humble servant leadership means seeking God's way.

Inspiration for this poem came from viewing a video from the Living Waters website of resort owner Larry Law, showing him being awarded the prestigious Chinese Canadian Entrepreneurship award for 2021–2022.

"*Instead, whoever wants to become great among you must be your servant, and whoever wants to be first must be your slave—just as the Son of Man did not come to be served, but to serve, and to give his life as a ransom for many*" (Mathew 20:26b–28).

Virtues to Value

At the end of your life, what matters most?
Will friends and family your success toast?
Or will you be remembered for your love?

Resume virtues include career skills,
Strategies for success, marketplace thrills,
Your accomplishments highlighted as strengths.

Eulogy virtues, on the other hand,
Share character traits and influence grand,
Like your kindness, courage, honesty, faith.

Beware what kind of virtues to value,
As decade upon decade you pass through,
Because, in the end, what counts is love's view!

Inspiration for this poem came from reading a blog post by Rich Janes, noting David Brook's comments on the tension between résumé virtues and eulogy virtues. See "The Moral Bucket List" dated April 12, 2015.[9]

---

[9] David Brooks, "The Moral Bucket List," *The New York Times*, April 11, 2015, https://www.nytimes.com/2015/04/12/opinion/sunday/david-brooks-the-moral-bucket-list.html?searchResultPosition=3.

Yoked with You

Like workhorses climbing a steep hill,
Lead horse shifts weight to avoid a spill.

Yoked with You, You give me strength and rest,
Yoked with You, I'm well-equipped and blessed,
Yoked with You, You call me to obey,
Yoked with You, Together we will pray:

> For your will to be done,
> Transformation proven;
> Forgiveness now begun,
> Seventy times seven;
> Love's release welcome,
> On earth as in heaven.

Like workhorses climbing a steep hill,
God carries me, to avoid a spill.

Inspiration for this poem came from an image of two workhorses yoked together; on steep-hill climbs, the lead horse would choose to shift the weight and carry more of the load if needed. I found this insight intriguing and applicable to our faith walk. When we are yoked with God, through the Holy Spirit, God knows our needs and our strength and constantly adjusts what we carry and what He carries.

Chapter 9
Trust

TABLE OF CONTENTS

Arising Capacity	152
Be in God to Fill Heart's Gap	153
Dignity's Mantle	154
Double Grace	155
Grace Gems	157
Imbedded	158
In Him	159
Lit Identity: I Am a Child of God (song)	160
Lit Identity: We are the Bride of Christ (song)	161
Lit Identity's Three Strands	162
Lit in Truth	163
Please Love	164
Thankfulness	165
Unfailing Love's Persistent Pursuit	166
Wellspring of God's Favour	167

Themes in this chapter include trust, identity, and grace.

Arising Capacity

Today, dear friend, let's STAR CAP a city
with

CAP   A   CITY
        TO LOVE
        TO TRUST
        TO SHINE TRUTH

Pray today for God to give His Spirit
     LOVE IN TRUST
     L   I   T
      Identity sparkling

Pray today for God to give His Spirit
     LOVE IN TRUTH
     L   I   T
      Identity sparkling
     TO SHINE TRUTH

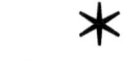

      ARISING
CAP   A   CITY

Be in God to Fill Heart's Gap

In God Alone, Peace
HEART'S   G A P   IS FILLED
God's Great PLAN: **BE IN GOD**!
B I G
GOD'S **BIG** PLAN
BE   G   IN
O
D
IN
BEGIN our BEGINNING
our ENDING,   bE IN GoD
E   N   D ING right where GOD wants us!
our INNER BEING, our LIT IDENTITY
FILLED WITH PEACE AND CONFIDENCE!
BE IN GOD
BE IN GOD
BE IN GOD

Inspiration for this poem came from a poem titled "Be in God Is God's Big Plan," published in Nancy (Warwick) Kingdon's earlier collection, *Humming Words* (2018).

Dignity's Mantle

acknowledging justice, acknowledging kindness,
as the mantle for mankind, ennobles, magnifies, enriches …

releasing humanity to believe
in a magnificent God beyond us,
in the hope for a better tomorrow,
in the power of an unchanging God.

releasing humanity to accept
our identity as God's children,
His sons and His daughters,
dignified, and made in His image!

Inspiration for this poem came from viewing the website for Living Waters in Collingwood, Ontario.

"*He has shown you, O mortal, what is good. And what does the Lord require of you? To act justly and to love mercy and to walk humbly with your God*" (Micah 6:8).

Double Grace

I have become mute, silent, without voice,
without words to proclaim God's majesty;
I bow my head and cry "Holy! Holy!"
my pounding heartbeat echoes drumming thoughts,
penetrating new, unfamiliar depths,
where untouchable, unknowable things
swim outside my reach, awakening me
to want something nameless, beyond my world;

carried along, I enter a vast realm
unfolding before me, but still shapeless,
impossible to describe using words,
yet my soul responds with strong emotion,
yearnings, hidden desires activated
to seek, to touch untouchable glory;
unworthy I am, and without merit,
except that I feel invited, welcomed

to step outside my world, outside myself,
drawn inside something new, I don't deserve;
still, I must obey and open my heart;
I must pray for courage, seek fearlessness
ready to expand beyond my limits,
as an act of trust, and worship, and love;
I feel like a moth mesmerized by light
entering, knowing I will die, I go.

believing that what I'll find must be faced
"yea, though He slay me, yet I will trust Him"
surfaces as a saying I once heard
spoken, written, or recalled from my past;
yet, once inside, I'm stunned, transformed;
I exit a butterfly painted bright
colours, my wings strong, carrying new joy.
my heart healed, my mind released to fight

endowed through the Spirit of wisdom
I have touched as I worship God's glory;
as true GRACE doubled again to: GRACE GRACE

G	Giver of all loving and good gifts,
R	Restorer of all that is broken,
A	Advocate of marginalized poor,
C	Creator of all that is worthy,
E	Equipping disciples to meet needs.

having asked for revelation, I go
forward on wings renewed to fly high,
awakening joy's new song, given grace
to know the name of the One I adore:
JESUS is His name—He reigns forever,
filling all of creation with His love,
able to defeat every enemy,
He reigns supreme—nothing impossible!

Inspiration for the concept of double grace—not spoken once, but twice, to reinforce it—came from grace message spoken by Rev. Rick Busse, Lead Pastor at Evangel Church in Oshawa, Ontario, on July 30, 2023.

"*Though he slay me, yet will I hope in him; I will surely defend my ways to his face*" (Job 13:15).

Grace Gems

GEMS polished to sparkling clean essence, glowing with vision's sheen;
GEMS grace-perfected, to meet God's design specifications;
GEMS like sapphire blues, rubies, emeralds, magnifications;
GEMS precious in God's sight, filling His heart with music's delight!

G	**E**	**M**	**S**
R	M	E	E
A	P	R	C
C	O	C	U
E	W	Y	R
undeserved;	E	withholding	E,
merit	R	sin's	ready
is	E	punishment;	to
mine!	D		answer
	strength		His
	to		call!
	obey		
	God's		
	will!		

Imbedded

Our story is imbedded,
That's right, imbedded!

In Christ Jesus' love story
Wherever we're headed!

Our story is imbedded,
Alive in His HISTORY,

His Story Surrounding us,
Our story deep inside His!

In Him

In Him, in Him, in Him,
   In His Blood Identity as Messiah
      In HIM,
         I STAND FIRM,
            VICTORIOUS forever, over
               all accusations from Satan!

Lit Identity: I Am a Child of God
(song)

Listen now to God's Word:
You are a child of God.
Remember: God loves You!

Hear now the truth of God's Word:
You are a love child of God!
Rejoice! God REALLY loves You!

Sing with me, sing with me, our song of joy:
I am a love child of God, truly loved!
His Inheritance I am, TRULY LOVED!

Lit Identity: We are the Bride of Christ
(song)

Listen now to God's Word:
We are the Bride of Christ.
Rejoice! Jesus loves Us!

Hear now the truth of God's Word:
We are Jesus' chosen Bride;
Jesus REALLY does love us!

Sing with us, sing with us our song of joy:
We are Jesus' precious Bride, truly loved!
His Inheritance we are, TRULY LOVED!

"*As a young man marries a young woman, so will your Builder marry you; as a bridegroom rejoices over his bride, so will your God rejoice over you*" (Isaiah 62:5).

Lit Identity's Three Strands

ribbons of Love in Truth,
hide Lit identity inside TRUST;

trust in hearts frames TRUTH;
truth in hearts claims TRUST;
love in hearts tames LOVE;

trust in truth—severs sin's shame;
love in truth—conquers condemnation's blame;
till our lit identity reflects Jesus' name!

Lit in Truth

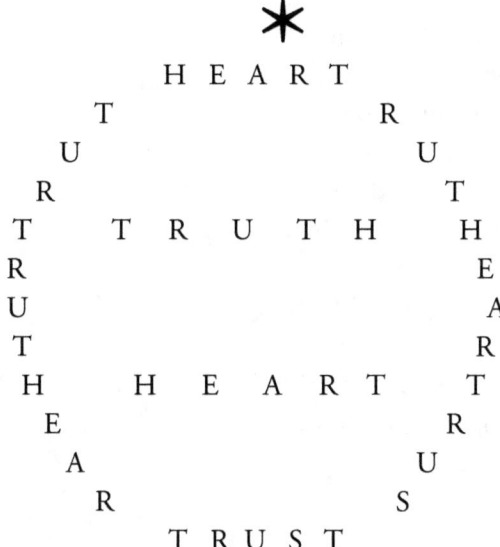

CHAPTER 9: TRUST

Please Love

P	Promise, without forgetting;
L	Listen, without interrupting;
E	Enjoy, without complaint;
A	Answer, without arguing;
S	Share, without pretending;
E	Enjoy giving, without sparing;
L	Learn to love all; pray without ceasing;
O	Open your heart to love always;
V	Vow to forgive, without punishing;
E	Enjoy trusting, without wavering.

Inspiration for this poem came from a poster titled "Touching Hearts" that I saw on a friend's website. It lists ten ways to love. I redesigned it, adding my own thoughts, to create this poem titled "Please Love."

Thankfulness

out of a thankful heart
        flows
                love of God,

out of a thankful heart
        glows
                truth of God,

out of a thankful heart
        shows
                trust of God,

out of a thankful heart
        blows
                perfumed prayers of peace

out of a thankful heart
        throws
                unending showers of praise,

out of a thankful heart
        sows
                bowers of awakening,

out of a thankful heart
        arose
                limitless powers of grace.

Unfailing Love's Persistent Pursuit

All around I hear loud commotions,
Yet I climb mountainsides and swim oceans,
Because of Your unfailing love, dear God.

All around I see earthquakes, wars, danger,
Yet I embrace baby in a manger,
Feeling God's promise of unfailing love!

All around I smell burning signs of times,
Yet I rest in sweet fragrance of green pines,
Like scent of God's unfailing love Presence!

All around I watch unfolding touch-taste
Feast tables of God's Word pleading for haste,
Responses from shattered hearts needing love!

All around I trust unseen grace at play,
Chasing after children, tagging God's way,
As multitudes find God's unfailing love!

Wellspring of God's Favour

Do you want unending blessings to last?
God has strength to give life to those who ask!

Through His unfailing love, in God we trust,
Through God's grace, into His favour we're thrust!

God's favour is the supreme cause of joy,
His greatest blessing now ours to enjoy!

Knowing God's love and feeling His Presence,
Ignites well-spring of divine love's presents!

God's favour surrounds the righteous with peace,
Joy's unending blessings will never cease!

"Surely you have granted him unending blessings and made him glad, with the joy of your presence" (Psalm 21:6).

"Surely, Lord, you bless the righteous; you surround them with your favour as with a shield" (Psalm 5:12).

Chapter 10

Strength

TABLE OF CONTENTS

Firefly Ribbons of Worship	170
God's Favour	171
Heart Songs	172
Inside Heart's Halls	173
Lamp Stand Prayer	174
Living Water (song)	175
Majesty	176
New Year's Day Prayer	177
Paradise: A Walled, Well-Watered Garden	178
Show Me How	179
Soaring Wings	180
Song of Rejoicing (song)	181
Streams of Abundant Life	182
This Stroll Inside a Rose Garden	183
Worship's Raindrops	184

Themes in this chapter include strength, songs, and worship.

Firefly Ribbons of Worship

Holy Spirit, I am in awe of You …
this day I praise You for time together,
understanding's joy, peace flowing through me,
refreshing blessings, like rain showers, blow
breezes of rejoicing, our hearts aligned,
your river of life streaming hope's ribbon—
waving sparkling beauty, like a banner
blessing our land, unfurling renewal!
I'm given a place to stand, believe, wait—
knowing belonging's house is being built,
hearts are being mended, repaired, healed,
promises on their way, coming, coming
awe, a wonderland of worship coming;
playful poetic images flood me,
thoughts, like darting firefly comets, delight
my soul, igniting songs of rejoicing,
as heaven becomes my soul's dwelling place,
and prayer carries me beyond all limits.

God's Favour

God's favour, like a wellspring
Releases blessings to flow;
God's Presence brings rejoicing,
Moving through us, fast or slow;
Remember to always pray,
Ask for God's favour today;
His Presence will guide you true,
Carrying you always through
Every temptation and trial,
Hour by hour, mile after mile;
Flowing conduit you'll be,
Pouring out eternity,
For out of God's heart above
Favour comes—His Presence's love!

"*Surely you have granted him unending blessings and made him glad with the joy of your presence*" (Psalm 21:6).

"Moses said to the Lord, 'See, you say to me, "Bring up this people," but you have not let me know whom you will send with me. Yet you have said, "I know you by name, and you have also found favor in my sight."' And he said, 'My presence will go with you, and I will give you rest.' … And he said to him, 'If your presence will not go with me, do not bring us up from here.' … And the Lord said to Moses, 'This very thing that you have spoken I will do, for you have found favor in my sight, and I know you by name'" (Exodus 33:12, 14–15, 17, ESV).

Heart Songs

H   Hallelujah! Praise the Lord!
E   Every heart bows to Jesus!
A   Amen, sings my heart, Amen!
R   Rejoice always! NOW Rejoice!
T   Trusting in God satisfies hearts!

S   Songs of rejoicing we sing!
O   Oneness of heart, God will bring!
N   Never stop wanting God's way!
G   Grace flows, when we learn to pray!
S   Sing heart songs, ADORING our King!

Inside Heart's Halls

Inside your heart's halls,
        scrolled on your heart's walls
Are thoughts that guide you,
        wisdom's words to woo
You close, healing much
        with holiness's touch—
Yet, it is your choice
        to nourish this voice,
Wonder flowing true,
        worship lit in you!

What poem, song, is etched?
        What memory is sketched?
What words are scrolled?
        Spirit-fed, controlled?
Radiating truth,
        penetrating proof
Like prayerful thought's twirls,
        calligraphy's swirls,
Paint poems of love,
        poured out from above!

Describe your heart's space—
        is it full of grace?
Is your heart a place,
        reflecting God's face?
Lessons He's taught you,
        like pondering's dew?
Guiding your footsteps;
        wiped, paid-in-full debts?
Is your heart made right,
        awesome joy's delight?

Lamp Stand Prayer

L	**L**ight of the gospel be our song today;
A	**A**mazing joy of the Lord be our strength;
M	**M**ercy of the Lord make true healing stay;
P	**P**resence of the Lord stretching hope's length.
S	**S**ecure peace, be our resting place today;
T	**T**ruth from God's Word, shine Your light now in us;
A	**A**rmour-clad we go safely on our way,
N	**N**ourished to soar high into God's purpose,
D	**D**elight's song our motivation to pray.

Living Water
(song)

With joy you will draw water
From the wells of salvation,
From the wells of salvation!

With joy you will find Jesus,
The spring of living water,
The spring of living water!

Refreshed, drink living water
Jesus, the fountain of life
Jesus, the fountain of life!

"*With joy you will draw water from the wells of salvation*" (Isaiah 12:3).

"*For with you is the fountain of life; in your light we see light*" (Psalm 36:9).

"*My people have committed two sins: They have forsaken me, the spring of living water, and they have dug their own cisterns, broken cisterns that cannot hold water*" (Jeremiah 2:13).

Majesty

grasping Jesus' majesty,
like flower freshly budding
slowly, slowly awakens,
petals, soft pink lips, moving
hearts to whisper in wonder,
breath's mist exhaling worship,
raising, raising oneness's hearts
to reach up, seeking beyond
known places, beyond patterns,
into unexplored spaces,
belonging's voice beckoning
hearts to prayerfully enter,
laying down all that we are,
to become a new creation.

"*Therefore, if anyone is in Christ, the new creation has come: The old has gone, the new is here!*" (2 Corinthians 5:17).

New Year's Day Prayer

It is New Year's Day. Thank You for taking the old me and covering me over in the blood of Christ, and wrapping me in the armour of God, and causing me to arise anew, arise afresh, cleansed, made whole, made holy, and able to enter Your Presence uninhibited, without barrier, fear, stain, or pain.

>Today, I now
>arise into a new day,
>arise into a new way,
>rejoicing always as I learn to pray,
>>to play,
>>to stay
>
>near to You, wanting what You want for me,
>all of the desires of my heart aligned into the desires in your heart for me!
>Today, I am blessed beyond all measure, with a glorious year ahead unfolding!
>Today, and in the year ahead, God's goodness, grace, greatness will be revealed through me.
>May it be so, dear God, for me and for all those around me who seek to know You better!
>May Your love shine through me, and them, as light, drawing many closer to faith in Christ
>Jesus as Lord! Amen!

Inspiration for this poem came from notes from my devotional prayer journal on January 1, 2023.

Paradise: A Walled, Well-Watered Garden

Imagine coming by invitation,
To secret garden, air perfumed with scents,
Of roses, magenta-coloured blossoms,
Daisies with black eyes, skin soft, blonde hair loose.

This garden space, walled and well-watered,
To create lushness of greens and tall trees
Offering canopied shade paths of leaves,
Leading to fountain sprays and gentle streams.

It is here I walk with my Father God,
Meeting Him each morning, enjoying dawn
Together, my ears ready to listen,
Melody mists like prayers that glisten.

Hope's promises, blessings overflowing,
Unrestricted, limitless as God's love—
Allowing me this time in His Presence
Warms my heart, like Paradise's essence!

Show Me How

Show Me How to	Serve	You with a pure, clean heart,
		I pray, dear God;
	Satisfy	You with my art,
Show Me how to	Seek	You, telling our story
	Showcase	You, full of glory
Show Me How to	Serenade	You, songbird's glade
		I pray, dear God;
	Shower	You with thanksgiving's parade!

Soaring Wings

S	Soaring Wings lift me higher, higher, higher, to see what God reveals as His plan;
O	Oh, that my eyes might see, my ears might hear, my voice might speak of God's SALVATION for man!
A	Anointing love's power released,
R	Revelation's insight increased,
I	Inspiration given, awakening hope,
N	Never-ending faith soaring, vision's fresh scope;
G	Grace so divine, healed eyes, holiness seeing;
W	Wonder, causing worship to flood all our being,
I	Igniting our imagination with pure delight,
N	Night skies scrolling lit messages of revealed truth's light,
G	Gladness like shooting stars lifting wings wide-deep-high-long,
S	Soaring awe's wings proclaiming love's authority strong!

Song of Rejoicing
(song)

Hallelujah, what a Saviour!
Hallelujah, what a friend!
Hallelujah, God is with us,
With us now and to the end!

Victorious, flowing blessings,
Victorious, what a life!
Victorious beyond measure,
God's love, conquering all strife!

Celebration, enemies gone,
Celebration, what relief!
Celebration, rejoicing's great,
As faith flourishes through belief!

Streams of Abundant Life

H	Hearts of kindness all worshipping God, hovering	H
U		U
M	Minds of leadership vision, God magnifying	M
M		M
I		I
N		N
G		G
	WORDS OF LIFE	
B	Bodies healed—Church glorifying God—Belonging!	B
I		I
R		R
D		D
S	Souls lit, with wisdom's streams of life sparkling,	S

      E   Excellence   E   Encouragement
      V   Vision   V   Vespers
      O   Oneness   O   Openness
      K   Kindness   K   Knowledge
      E   Exaltation   E   Empowerment

STREAMS OF ABUNDANT LIFE
satisfying souls

Inspiration for this poem came from my earlier collection of poetry titled *Humming Words: Collection of Poetry* (2018) in which some poems encourage the reader "to pray, hovering before God in awe and worship."

This Stroll Inside a Rose Garden

in Your Presence, Lord,
        is deep satisfaction,
like a stroll with you
        inside a rose garden,
soft petals, fragrance,
        bright blue butterfly wings,
whispering wonder
        mingling pure awe's moments
with sweet contentment,
        soft breaths of belonging,
mixed with magical
        notes—heartfelt melodies,
beckoning me near
        my soul healed, made whole
overflowing joy
        tears unforgettable,
this stroll in garden
        S   Sparkling
        T   Trusting
        R   Rejoicing
        O   Obeying
        L   Listening
        L   Loving
this stroll in garden
        anointed satisfaction!

Worship's Raindrops

What's lovely worship?
        magnifying God,
        opening our heart,
        igniting love's start!

Think of a chapel,
        place of joyful praise,
        where freedom has come,
        faith's fullness now won!

Imagine beauty,
        satisfaction near,
        raindrops like bead drops,
        daintily meet needs!

INDEX

Abiding's Embrace (song)	62	Credit Account	136
Answered Prayer	2	Deliver Us Today, I Pray!	101
Answering God's Call	132	Dignity's Mantle	154
Arising Capacity	152	Disciple's Prayer	137
Be in God to Fill Heart's Gap	153	Divine Hope	80
Beware Bitter Roots	18	Do You Love Me?	138
Blessings Poured Out	63	Double Grace	155-156
Breath of Life Celebrated	64	Each One Caring	66
Breathing In and Out	63	Easter's Story	67
Building a Dwelling Place	97	Eight Characteristics of Christlikeness	139-140
Building Bible College Capacity	38-39	Emergency Numbers: The Traveller's Psalm	24
Building Capacity in Canada Part 1, Part 2	133-134	Empowerment	116
Call to Repentance	135	Erasing Sin Through Grace	102
Calling on the Name of the Lord God Almighty	78	Eternity's Choice	141-142
Caring Friends	3	Expand Belief	4
Cathedral Space: A Heart Song of Deep Spiritual Longing	79	Faith Matters	5
		Faith Seeds Growing	6
Celebrating ESL Ministry Launch	40-41	Faith Seeds Planted	81
Celebrating Sparkling Snow Bees	98-99	Faith Takes Action	7
Chapel Songs	100	Faith's Chairlift	8
Church Contemplations: Unity	114	Firefly Ribbons of Worship	170
Come, Holy Spirit!	65	Flowing River of Life	68
Contemplating Part 1: God's Seven Promises to Jacob	19	Free from Fear and Anxiety	82
		Fruit of the Spirit	69
Contemplating Part 2: Jacob's Seven Responses to God	20-21	Giving Kindness	9
		God is Love	42
Contemplating the New Covenant Part 1	22	God's Favour	171
Contemplating the New Covenant Part 2	23	God's Growth Promises	25
Creative Vowels	115	God's Inheritance	43

Grace Gems	157	Living Water (song)	175
Gratitude's Heart Song	70	Love Empowered Offspring	51
Grow in Power	117	Maggie's Place Beckons: Come!	52-53
Grow Your Church Today, Dear God	44	Majestic Melodies in Motion	124
Growth Track Steps	45	Majesty	176
Healing Our Land	71	Meet Magnolia Maggie	54-55
Healing Place	46	Mentors Impact the Next Generation	144
Heart Songs	172	Mobilizing a Mentoring Movement	145
Hearts Holding Holiness	103	Mouths Glowing Hope	87
Hearts Set Free	104	New Year's Day Prayer	177
Hope's Oneness of Heart	118-119	One Single Moment	106
Hope's Radiance	120	Oneness Arising	125
Hospitality's Power	26	Oneness's Waves	126
Igniting Lit Identity Through Pondering Name of Jesus	121	Paradise: A Walled, Well-watered Garden	178
		Path of Righteousness (song)	88
Imbedded	158	Paths of Peace	107
In Him	159	Pathways of Peace	89
In Your Presence	72	Perfumed Vessels	27
Infinite Love	122	Please Love	164
Inside Heart's Halls	173	Polished Beach Glass Hearts	108
Intimacy with God	123	Powerful Prayer of Unquantifiable Love	56-57
Jars of Clay	143	Prayerful Preserve Jars	90
Jesus' Name	83	Proof Requested	127
Joy Path Felt: My Prayer for You Today	84	Purposefully Rewarded	28
Lamp Stand Prayer	174	Radar, Rodney's Bear	146
Launching ESL Ministry	47	Reflections on Cities Made Whole	91
Lessons from Jabez	10	Rooms to Explore	128
Life's Greatest Question	73	Sabbath Rest (The)	11
Light of Truth	85	Sanctuary Space	12
Light Shines Through	105	Seeking God	13
Limitlessness	48-50	Servant Leadership	147
Lit Identity: I Am the Child of God (song)	160	Shake Up Our World Through Servanthood Attitudes	109
		Shocking Authority Part 1	29
Lit Identity: We are the Bride of Christ (song)	161	Shocking Authority Part 2	30
		Show Me How	174
Lit Identity's Three Strands	162	Soaring Wings	180
Lit in God's Sight	86	Solitude: What Is It?	14
Lit in Truth	163		

Song of Rejoicing (song)	181
Streams of Abundant Life	182
Thankfulness	165
This Stroll Inside a Rose Garden	183
To Love and Be Loved	110
Tree of Life Called Wisdom (Parts 1, 2, 3)	31-33
Trusting God Through Change	34
Truth Wrestles Lies to the Ground	111-112
Twenty Words	15
Unfailing Love's Persistent Pursuit	166
Uniting All	129
Virtues to Value	148
Vision's Footsteps	16
We Are Your Fruit	58
Wedding of the Lamb	74
Wellspring of God's Favour	167
Wisdom and Revelation	92
Wisdom's Path	75
Word of God	35
Worship's Raindrops	184
Yoked With You	149
You Are My Beloved	59
Zesty Fruit of the Spirit	76

Appendix

MEDITATIVE REFLECTIONS ON 150 FAITH WALK POEMS

In a blank notebook, start your personal prayer-poetry writing journal. Write answers in your journal either for your personal spiritual growth or for scheduled discussions with others, such as your spiritual mentor, your spiritual growth/ Bible study group, or your devotional poetry writing group. Everyone is called to be a witness to what Jesus Christ has done in their lives. This meditative faith walk journal is intended to help you expand your faith journey's voice!

Chapter 1: Faith

1. "Answered Prayer"
   Describe what it means to you personally when you ponder "together our prayers, like chain roots long stretch from one heart to another, so strong God's Presence of grace is felt in garden, as every prayer's answered: "Yes and amen!"
2. "Caring Friends"
   Discuss what it means to you to depend on God through prayer. Do you agree/disagree with the following two statements and why?
   a) "When we carry others, or are carried, we humble ourselves to depend on God; prayer builds a caring community, connecting us with God and one another."
   b) "But no extended warranties exist to frame wishes into reality."
3. "Expand Belief"
   What does "expand belief in Christ Jesus" mean to you today? Write your own poem or acrostic poem, using either BELIEF or EXPAND as the first letter for each line, with seven to ten syllables chosen, to describe what this theme means to you.
4. "Faith Matters"
   Discuss in a few sentences (one hundred words or less) why faith matters to you, and share your understanding of the verse "*If you do not stand firm in your faith, you will not stand at all.*"

5. "Faith Seeds Growing"

    Ponder and write out your response to the following: What are faith's seeds in your life, and how can you help them to grow?

6. "Faith Takes Action"

    What do you need to take action on today, as a declaration of faith? Speak it aloud. Write it down. Share it with a trustworthy friend, and pray for wisdom to move forward, able with confidence to take the action you feel God wants you to take.

7. "Faith's Chair Lift"

    How can you be faith's chair lift today, for someone near you? What specifically can you do, or pray, or give to become that strength to a loved one? Have you asked God for wisdom today to become His chair lift, for someone dear to you?

8. "Giving Kindness"

    Has someone's kind deed blessed you or touched your heart in a special way? When have you been an unsung hero, giving an act of kindness to another that somehow made a difference?

9. "Lessons from Jabez"

    Do you have a hurtful "label" that you must overcome—an unkind memory about yourself? Learn from Jabez how to pray and receive deliverance from this lie, this hurtful label, that needs to be severed from your identity and thoughts about yourself. Be healed! Ask God for help to receive this healing He wants to give to you!

10. "The Sabbath Rest"

    What does it mean to you to enter Jesus' gift of a Sabbath rest? Are you ready to receive this gift? What keeps you from accepting this gift if you're not yet ready?

11. "Sanctuary Space"

    What sanctuary space are you seeking to enter, or are able to enter, today? How would you describe your life purpose? What is happening in your life right now that helps move you toward fulfilling your life purpose?

12. "Seeking God"

    What does it look like for you to seek and please God? Is this a new idea, or has it been spoken to you again and again during the past year, or even decade?

13. "Solitude: What Is It?"

    What is your understanding of solitude? Why pursue it?

14. "Twenty Words, Lord"

    Describe how a mere twenty-word prayer, by God's grace, has the potential power to "protect us and our loved ones from hell." Are you praying this prayer for yourself and your family?

15. "Vision's Footsteps"

    Contemplate the fifteen "I" words and identify which ones resonate most with you personally. Note whether visions, vespers, or voices draw you most, and explain why you chose each word. Try writing a personal creative poem or devotional on this theme.

Chapter 2: Authority

1. "Beware Bitter Roots"

    What do you do if you have bitter roots? Do you have any that you need to acknowledge, and ask for help to let go of, receiving the grace of God's healing? Ask God to reveal to you any hidden roots that need to be dealt with.

2. "Contemplating, Part 1, God's Seven Promises to Jacob"

    Reread the seven promises to Jacob. Has God given promises to you? What are they? Have all been fulfilled yet, or are some still to come? Which of Jacob's promises resonate most with you as your desire?

3. "Contemplating, Part 2, Jacob's Seven Responses to God"

    Which of Jacob's responses resonate most with you? Have you responded to God's voice in a similar way, or is this something you plan to do in the near future? Pray about each response, and ask God to help you see whether He wants you to catch hold of any new insight or plan for tomorrow.

4. "Contemplating the New Covenant, Part 1"

    What laws has God put in your heart and mind?

5. "Contemplating the New Covenant, Part 2"

    Which of the seven measurable outcomes of knowing Jesus and His new covenant are you personally experiencing?

6. "Emergency Numbers: The Traveller's Psalm"

    When was the last time you travelled somewhere and prayed the words of Psalm 121, acknowledging God's protection over you?

7. "God's Growth Promises"

    Which of God's growth promises resonate most with you?

8. "Hospitality's Power"

    When was the last time you had a difficult confrontation to deal with, and you sat down—or did not sit down—with that person, ready to share food before both of you? How did this problem get resolved, or is it still unresolved? Any thoughts about adding hospitality as a future value when facing a difficult confrontation?

9. "Perfumed Vessels"

What do you think helps us breath in, then out, God's perfumed love?

10. "Purposefully Rewarded"

In what way does God's promise to reward all for what they have done impact you personally? Any added thoughts on this?

11. "Shocking Authority, Part 1"

In what way is God's authority shocking in your life or the lives of those close to you?

12. "Shocking Authority, Part 2"

What impossible things, such as miracles, has God done in your life or in the lives of those close to you? Who have you shared this blessing with?

13. "Tree of Life Called Wisdom, Parts 1, 2, 3"

Which adjective (happy, joyful, blessed) do you prefer when you contemplate wisdom, and why? Why do you think wisdom is so important and the theme of so many verses in Proverbs?

14. "Trusting God Through Change"

Are you trusting God wholeheartedly through the trials and changes in your life, or are you struggling to do so? Why is this such a hard battle at times?

15. "Word of God"

Have you asked God for wisdom today, to better understand His Word? What insights or spiritual revelations have you received that have impacted your life in some new way? Please write these insights down in your prayer journal.

Chapter 3: Inheritance

1. "Building Bible College Capacity"

Have you prayed today for both leadership and students of a Bible college you know? Ask God if there is anything else you need to do, such as supporting a Bible college ministry or encouraging a student to consider attending Bible college. Ask God to send workers into the harvest field.

2. "Celebrating ESL Ministry Launch"

Pray for this ministry. Ask God if He would have you involved in an ESL ministry launch at your church or community.

3. "God Is Love"

    How have you been transformed by God's love? Write a sentence or two that could be shared with your children, grandchildren, or other young people in your life. Plan to make copies and attach it to the next birthday card you give them!

4. "God's Inheritance"

    Write out one to three examples of great things God has done in your life.

5. "Grow Your Church Today, Dear God"

    What is one favourite "word of faith" or scripture verse that you love to hold on to and use for meditation?

6. "Growth Track Steps"

    How can churches foster safe community? How can people be encouraged to know their spiritual purpose?

7. "Healing Place"

    How can our churches become stronger healing places? Identify three potential barriers to this happening and then write out three prayers to combat these barriers.

8. "Launching ESL Ministry"

    What ministries are you involved with in your church that help "faith take flight"? What is your action plan for the next twelve months?

9. "Limitlessness"

    Describe as many attributes of God as you can, and describe *who* God is, in your experience, and what specific ways you have seen Him transform lives around you.

10. "Love-Empowered Offspring"

    How are you God's oil lamp and His dream-come-true? Thank God now for helping you to be pleasing in His sight!

11. "Maggie's Place Beckons: Come!"

    How are your eyes fixed on Jesus? How are you "alive in mercy" and able to walk in grace-empowered mercy? What makes this faith development journey difficult?

12. "Meet Magnolia Maggie"

    Who do you need to forgive, or to focus on building up and being kind toward? Ask God for divine help and strength. God can change your heart and control your emotions if you have trouble letting go of unforgiveness. Ask Him now!

13. "Powerful Prayer of Unquantifiable Love"

    Ask God to strengthen you with power so that Christ may dwell in your heart, leading and guiding you to do what pleases God.

14. "We Are Your Fruit"

    Are you being mentored, or mentoring others, so that you're either the fruit of their labour, or others are the fruit of your prayer and discipleship labour? Ask God to deepen your faith roots and help you encourage someone else to deepen their faith roots.

15. "You Are My Beloved"

    Meditate on the endearments listed in this poem, as if God's voice was being whispered in your ear, and then write your own response to God in a poem, prayer, love letter, or song for His ear alone. Be specific. Make it personal. Tell Him how much you love Him!

Chapter 4: Transformation

1. "Abiding's Embrace" (song)

    Imagine grace forests, tall and beautiful, and then see yourself abiding in the shade of these leaves, resting and in perfect peace. What would you tell God if the two of you were sitting here together, on a bench, looking at the lofty evergreens, enjoying the filtered light through the trees, and smelling the pine, the spruce, the honeysuckle, the sweet aromas of stillness and sun-bathed nature? Open your heart and share what you are feeling. God wants a closer and deeper intimacy of shared feelings and thoughts with you; He longs to hear you speak to Him and choose to pour out prayers and praises.

2. "Blessings Poured Out"

    Make a commitment to make thanksgiving your heart's focus for a twenty-four-hour period; start by writing out twenty to thirty blessings you can be thankful for as your heart begins to swell with praise and thanksgiving.

3. "Breath of Life Celebrated"

    Search your memory for twenty to thirty smiling faces, praying over each of these individuals with a thankful heart for all that God has done, and for the joy of knowing them, if even for a single day or occasion.

4. "Come, Holy Spirit!"

    How have you been equipped to do God's will? What has God been teaching you today, or this week, or this month?

5. "Each One Caring"

    Describe what God's "cathedral heart space" means to you and ask Him to help you see this space more clearly, through His vision and thoughts. Ask God to expand your understanding of worship and the "healed heart space" He wants you to joyfully experience. If possible, picture a real place, such as garden, that you delight to visit. Thank God for this treasure, this place, this memory, this "happy heart space."

6. "Easter's Story"

    What does it mean to enter God's Sabbath rest? How does the Easter story relate to this?

7. "Flowing River of Life"

    What does "flowing grace" mean to you, and what has God delivered you from, or healed you from, that allows you increased freedom from former bondages or restrictions?

8. "Fruit of the Spirit"

    Pray now for God to have His way in you, forming, reforming, unforming, informing, transforming you, till the fruit of the Spirit grows in you, unhindered, and you are better equipped to serve God as His disciple and disciple-maker. Then ask Him to reveal what work He has just done in you to make you ready to serve Him. Join God in the movement of His Spirit that He is inviting you into as your new faith journey focus.

9. "Gratitude's Heart Song"

    Ask God for a heart of gratitude and for His help to hold on to this attitude of gratitude.

10. "Healing Our Land"

    Meditate on what it means to be *forceful* and choose one idea to focus on for the coming week, praying, fasting, and seeking to learn more about this area.

11. "In Your Presence"

    In what specific ways has your life changed because Jesus lives? Ponder these blessings and praise God for His amazing Presence.

12. "Life's Greatest Question"

    Ask God for help to see others through His eyes, and yourself through His eyes, and then try to answer the question: "How much joy did you give today, this week, this month, this year to someone?" Try to respond with specific illustrations.

13. "Wedding of the Lamb"

    Why do you think Jesus chose the name "Lamb" for his wedding day? Why do you think He valued this name above all others He could have chosen?

14. "Wisdom's Path"

    Contemplate wisdom, rereading Psalms 1–7 if desired, then ask God to help you pursue and receive wisdom as He teaches you more about why wisdom matters.

15. "Zesty Fruit of the Spirit"

    Contemplate the fruit of the Spirit, rereading Galatians 5. Then ask God for increased fruitfulness.

Chapter 5: Hope

1. "Calling on the Name of the Lord God Almighty"

    Pray that God will revive us so that we can call on the Name of the Lord. Pray for salvation for all in your family, circle of friends, and neighbours who don't know Jesus as Lord and Saviour. Write out three to five miracles God has already done in your life. Ask God for more miracles and to open your eyes to recognize more miracles He has done.

2. "Cathedral Space: A Heartsong of Deep Spiritual Longing"

    Think about what your heart longs for, and pray for these things now. **What** scripture, images, thoughts cause you to enter into an attitude of awe, wonder, and praise? Consider **Why? When? Where? How? Who** is with you? Jot down your thoughts.

3. "Divine Hope"

    What revealed and released images or insights about the kingdom of God have you received, or heard from others, that you can rejoice over and add to your prayer journal?

4. "Faith Seeds Planted"

    Why is it impossible to please God without faith? How does planting and nurturing faith roots please God?

5. "Free from Fear and Anxiety"

    What happens when someone is consumed by fear and anxiety? What situations cause you to fear or feel anxious? How can you overcome these things?

6. "Jesus' Name"

    What "new hope" has begun in your life through embracing the name of Jesus? How has Jesus helped you to overcome past temptations or former strongholds of sin?

7. "Joy Path Felt: My Prayer Today for You"

    On a scale of one to ten, how much joy do you think you have? Why or why not? Challenge: What can you do differently to bring more joy into your life? Have you prayed this week for joy to increase in the hearts of your children and loved ones?

8. "Light of Truth"

    How does God's Word impact the level of faith each one of us has or wants to have? Are you satisfied with the weekly amount of time you spend reading scripture? Ask God to help you commit to a Bible reading action plan for the coming week.

9. "Lit in God's Sight"

    Are there any desires in your heart that you need to submit? If so, ask God to help you and to align your desires with the desires in His heart.

10. "Mouths Glowing Hope"

    List three to five goals that you think would increase godliness and glorify God?

11. "Path of Righteousness"

    Contemplate Proverbs 4:18 (NIV): "*The path of righteousness is like the morning sun, shining ever brighter until the full light of day.*" What does this mean to you?

12. "Pathways to Peace"

    What words of scripture do you want to meditate on today, this week, this month? Create a checklist of verses for the coming season.

13. "Prayerful Preserve Jars"

    What verses, in your opinion, are salt-shaker words, empowered to help heal someone in need of God's counsel? Create a list of three to five instructional verses.

14. "Reflections on Cities Made Whole"

    What prayer words would you use to build up people living in your city? What encouraging scripture verse comes to your mind?

15. "Wisdom and Revelation"

    Ask God today for the spirit of both wisdom and revelation, because He invites us to ask Him for both gifts! Have you received divine revelation in the past that has helped you see a situation through fresh eyes and insight? If so, write about it in your prayer journal.

Chapter 6: Restoration

1. "Breathing In and Out"

    Prayerfully contemplate answers before responding. What five values are you breathing in today, and what five discards are you breathing out, to release and let go?

2. "Building a Dwelling Place"

    Pray for wisdom to answer the next question truthfully. Is your spiritual dwelling place inside or outside the heart of God and His divine purpose for your life? Do you know your purpose? If so, what is it? If not, pray for ears to hear and eyes to see what God wants you to receive as His blessing.

3. "Celebrating Sparkling Snow Bees"

    Does this image of a cloud of white lights, lifting and moving like a swarm of snow bees, speak to your heart? If so, write your story. If not, write in your journal about any kind of spiritual dream or image that has special meaning for you, something that delights you in some way. Ask God what He wants you to do with that lovely image.

4. "Chapel Songs"

    What are three promises of God that you would like released in your life?

5. "Deliver Us Today, I Pray!"

    In Psalm 32, we read of God surrounding us with songs of deliverance. What songs of deliverance are you praying to be released today?

6. "Erasing Sin Through Grace"

    What scripture verse "word swords" do you want to swing this day, cutting through sin's strongholds? What truth do you want to speak that has the power to slice through the lies of Satan? Write out scripture's "word swords" now.

7. "Hearts Holding Holiness"

    What is your understanding of sanctification, holiness, and godliness? Spend some time looking at scripture. What does the bible teach on these three subjects?

8. "Hearts Set Free"

    Think about the difference between hearts in bondage and hearts set free. Now rejoice that God is willing to set all captives free when they call out to Him and seek to obey His Word.

9. "Light Shines Through"

    How has God's Word shone through darkness in your life or the life of anyone close to you?

10. "One Single Moment"

    Take this moment to pray for someone or for something that matters to you, knowing that one single moment can make a life-changing difference. Be the spark God uses to release His miracle, His answer to our prayer, and His will to heal someone!

11. "Paths of Peace"

    Ponder God's gifts of mercy, power, and grace, and note what these words mean to you.

12. "Polished Beach Glass Hearts"

    Do you know any "beach glass women" who now are strong and healed and transformed, free from former shattered hearts, rejection, and brokenness? Praise and thank God for their healing testimonies and new life in Him!

13. "Shake Up Our World Through Servanthood Attitudes"

    What servanthood attitudes resonate most with you, and which are harder for you to do? Consider one individual you need to treat differently in the coming week and ask God for help to serve this person, connecting well.

14. "To Love and Be Loved"

    Make a list of those you love and those who love you back and thank God for each gift of His grace! Relationships need to be nourished. Nourish them by planning to do something nice for each one in the coming days.

15. "Truth Wrestles Lies to the Ground"

    If someone in your life is battling divorce, rejection, and the pain of low self esteem, pray for them. If you think it would help, send them this poem to encourage them to fight forces of evil trying to deepen rejection's lies!

Chapter 7: Oneness

1. "Church Contemplations: Unity"

    Describe your understanding of "unity through oneness of heart" and how this is lived out in the Christ-centric church setting.

2. "Creative Vowels"

    What is God's love story, alive in you? Write out this story in your prayer journal. Tell someone this story in the coming month.

3. "Empowerment"

    Pray for a move of God today, to open hearts to what He wants to do in our lives, in our families, in our churches, in our land, in our nation, in our world.

4. "Grow in Power"

   How does God's power shift the atmosphere?
5. "Hope's Oneness"

   How can our churches become better, more effective "houses of prayer"?
6. "Hope's Radiance"

   How does hope impact life for the better? Explore the difference between despair and hope, and how each one impacts our perceptions and beliefs.
7. "Igniting Lit Identity Through Pondering Name of Jesus"

   How does pondering the name of Jesus ignite spiritual understanding? Describe lit identity in as much detail as you can.
8. "Infinite Love"

   Describe your perception of Who God is and what Oneness is. Why does Oneness matter so much?
9. "Intimacy with God"

   Describe what you think intimacy with God looks and feels like. How intimate do you think your relationship with God is, in relation to others in your family or church? What can you do to increase your intimacy with God?
10. "Majestic Melodies in Motion"

    Describe your concept of oneness's majestic melodies in motion. Going where? Doing what? Sounding how? Engaging who? Experienced when?
11. "Oneness Arising"

    How does oneness open hearts, minds, and souls?
12. "Oneness's Waves"

    How can oneness act like a life preserver when life's waves are high and rough?
13. "Proof Requested"

    Pray today for God to heal our land and deliver us from evil influences.
14. "Rooms to Explore"

    Think about the rooms in God's heart and write your own story about exploring what you see, what you hear, and what God wants to share with you today.
15. "Uniting All"

    Why do you think Jesus prayed for Oneness, as His last prayer in John 17, for not only His disciples but those who would believe in Him later, in ages to come? No wonder Satan seeks to attack this value! Pray for God's help for all believers to stand firm in faith and in unity with God's Spirit, guiding us forward to do God's will.

Chapter 8: Obedience

1. "Answering God's Call"

    Do you have a book to write, a legacy story to tell? Do you know your spiritual gifts, and are you using them to further God's kingdom? Pray for God's direction now.

2. "Building Capacity in Canada, Part 1, Part 2"

    Please pray these prayers and invite others to join you, to pray with you these prayers for healing our nation of Canada!

3. "Call to Repentance"

    All of us are sinners. Humble yourself. What do you need to ask God to forgive you for today? Repent. Turn away from evil. Ask God for help to do things His way and to obey and please Him.

4. "Credit Account"

    Ask God to fill you with the desires in His heart for you, and to lay down any desires not of Him, so that you aren't hindered in your fulfillment of God's call on your life.

5. "Disciple's Prayer"

    Pray now as Jesus taught His disciples to pray.

6. "Do You Love Me?"

    Describe what you think it means to love Jesus.

7. "Eight Characteristics of Christlikeness"

    What aspect of Christlikeness speaks to your heart most from this list of eight characteristics? Why? What do you plan to do as follow-up?

8. "Eternity's Choice"

    Do you believe in God's love? Are you willing to commit to follow Jesus, and if so, what does that look like in terms of changes in how you presently live your life? If you haven't been baptized yet, are you willing to do so?

9. "Jars of Clay"

    How do justice and righteousness strengthen jars of clay?

10. "Mentors Impact the Next Generation"

    Who are you being mentored by, or who are you mentoring? If you're not doing so yet, are you willing to pray about this and seek to do so?

11. "Mobilizing a Mentoring Movement"

    Is mentoring a movement in your church? Pray for God's guidance in this area.

12. "Radar, Rodney's Bear"

    What treasured memory from your childhood or story do you want to tell your grandchildren or other young people in your life some day? Write it out.

13. "Servant Leadership"

    How are you serving God and others? Pray for guidance to articulate what God is asking you to do.

14. "Virtues to Values"

    Define "success" from a Christian perspective and from a worldly perspective and share what each means to you. What virtues do you value?

15. "Yoked With You"

    Describe what it means to be yoked to someone dear to you and also yoked to God Himself. Pray for God's wisdom to understand what it means to care for others in this way.

Chapter 9: Trust

1. "Arising Capacity"

    Pray for God to heal your city, granting truth and trust in God.

2. "Be in God to Fill Heart's Gap"

    Ask God for help to BEGIN in God, and END in God, always seeking to please and serve God, doing His will. Contemplate what this means to you.

3. "Dignity's Mantle"

    Why does focusing our eyes on Jesus instead of on people around us, or the world's views on things, make such a difference? Give some illustrations.

4. "Double Grace"

    Describe what God's grace means to you and how His grace has impacted your life in a personal way?

5. "Grace Gems"

    What visions has God given you recently? If you're not able to answer, pray for God's insight and for fresh visions that He wants you to hear, see, and be able to share as His purposes and direction.

6. "Imbedded"

    How is your life story imbedded into God's story and His history as revealed in His Word of truth?

7. "In Him"

    What accusations of Satan can you lay aside because of Jesus' victory and resurrection from death into life everlasting?

8. "Lit Identity: I Am the Child of God" (song)
   Have you asked God to give you ears to hear and eyes to see yourself through His understanding and voice, and His heart of love? Do so today. Ask also for your heart to open to believe what He reveals to you.
9. "Lit Identity: We are the Bride of Christ"
   When you look at your church and the people in your church, can you see them through God's eyes and love them, and together serve God with a joyful, unified spirit of oneness? If not, pray for God's healing and deliverance from whatever is separating you from them, and them from you. God is able to build you up into His dwelling place, where He is glorified. Amen.
10. "Lit Identity's Three Strands"
    Imagine your heart of love, your mind of truth, and your spirit of trust, fully healed from the world's voice of condemnation and contamination. Ask God to give you strength to trust His Word, to believe His promises, and to be free from the things that cause falsehood and destruction and bondages.
11. "Lit in Truth"
    Meditate for a while on the connectivity of three words: heart, truth, trust. Ask God for wisdom to catch hold of His design plan, to shine as His light as He weaves into us His understanding. Be awestruck by God's infinite loveliness!
12. "Please Love"
    Ask God to give you a heart of wisdom, to learn to love others as He wants you to do. This poem requires more than we are capable of, but with God, all things are possible. Acknowledge your need of His power and strength to be transformed into His design plan!
13. "Thankfulness"
    Perfume each day with a thankful heart, intentionally developing as a daily habit an attitude of gratitude. You may want to create a "thanksgiving praise calendar!"
14. "Unfailing Love: Persistent Pursuit"
    Do you need to take your eyes off the wars, rumours of wars, and destructive forces around us in today's world and fix your eyes on Jesus, trusting His promises and seeking to see the future through His declarations of a victorious future, with Him leading His people in His Holy Spirit's power? Ask God to take captive your thoughts and vision and help you to see life through His desires and spiritual perspective. Ask for a transformed mind.

15. "Wellspring of God's Favour"

    Think about God's favour and what it means to you. Thank God today for this amazing gift, this place where all other blessings originate.

Chapter 10: Strength

1. "Firefly Ribbons of Worship"

    As you bow your heart and head in worship today, put into your prayer journal your own song of praise, your own words of rejoicing, your own images of delight. Sing a song unto the Lord as your unique gift of thanksgiving unto your God, your Saviour, your Holy Spirit guiding you, your companion, and your heart's joy. Imagine your poem as a banner over your life, your home, your family!

2. "God's Favour"

    Do you know God's Presence today? If not, ask for God to reveal His Presence to you. If so, praise God for this blessing of His favour, and contemplate just how essential the Presence of God is in your life and in the lives of those around you.

3. "Heart Songs"

    Tell God today, this hour, how much you adore Him, love Him, and long to please Him. Write out your heart song and these words of adoration and worship.

4. "Inside Heart's Halls"

    What lessons has God taught you that you can share with someone you love? Record insights, lessons, and things that you know help guide you, encourage your heart, and will be worthwhile recording for future generations, or even your own meditations.

5. "Lamp Stand Prayer"

    What prayer do you want to hold on to and share with a loved one?

6. "Living Water" (song)

    What words do you want to drink in and receive as living water today? Ask God for help to BELIEVE these words and respond in faith, growing stronger faith roots today.

7. "Majesty"

    Have you laid down yourself and all that you think you are and invited God to have His way in your life, to make you a new creation? Expect transformation. Expect miracles! Expect to arise, set free!

8. "New Year's Day Prayer"
   Please pray the New Year's Day prayer for yourself today, and expect to see the next 365 days ahead blossom with God's Presence, Purpose, and Peace. Amen.
9. "Paradise: A Walled, Well-Watered, Garden"
   Contemplate the Presence of God as a fragrance and a grace garden of such beauty that you only marvel at God's goodness and glory. Open your heart now to worship this Giver of such bounty! Remember: as you draw near to God, He promises to draw near to you.
10. "Show Me How"
    Ask God for a voice to showcase His essence and what He has done in your life, so that you can be a lighthouse, a beacon of hope, a lit identity, able to radiate to others God's Presence in your life.
11. "Soaring Wings"
    How has God healed you? What images, imaginations, visions, discernments has He given to you that you want to put into writing or songs, to share with others?
12. "Song of Rejoicing"
    What BELIEF matters most to you right now, and what BELIEF do you want your loved ones to grasp, to take hold of, to rejoice over? Is it salvation through Jesus? Is it healing, received by faith? Is it God's revelation or vision given to you? Is it something else?
13. "Streams of Abundant Life"
    Have you learned to hover before God, in holiness and worship and awe? What stops you if you have not yet done so? What streams of abundant life are you rejoicing over this day, this week, this month because of God's goodness and grace?
14. "This Stroll Inside a Rose Garden"
    Write and share with someone the deep satisfaction you have experienced strolling in the garden of God's Presence.
15. "Worship's Raindrops"
    What wholeness of soul have you received through worship's raindrops, gently freeing you from former restraints? Describe what it means to you to walk confidently forward, set free from old patterns of thinking, able now to worship God in Spirit and in Truth?

Thank You, Lord, for this time of drawing close to You. Thank You for the divine gift of Your strength enabling us, as Your Church and Your inheritance, to arise on healing's wings! We are blessed beyond measure, and we *worship you*!

"*But for you who revere my name, the sun of righteousness will rise with healing in its rays. And you will go out and frolic like well-fed calves*" (Malachi 4:2).

Endorsements for Earlier Poetry Collections
(*Arising Rejoicing: A Collection of Devotional Poetry*)

Our Creator God enables some among us to create powerful emotions and images in our inner person that are rooted in eternal truth. Nancy (Warwick) Kingdon poetically does exactly that in her collection titled, *Arising Rejoicing: A Collection of Devotional Poetry*. My advice is to read slowly and ponder deeply.

—Rev. David Wells, General Superintendent,
The Pentecostal Assemblies of Canada (PAOC)

Nancy will creatively take you on a spiritual journey as you read and meditate on her anointed poetry. She has intentionally and wonderfully created eight chapters. You can use the chapter guide to locate where you are at a given stage of your adventure. Then she has prepared a creative, energetic, thoughtful feast of words and meditations that will feed your soul and rest your spirit. Bask in God's presence as you surround yourself with these life-giving words. You will want to keep this book handy and readily available. Use it as a companion and guide as you proceed on your spiritual way.

—Rev. Peter W. Cusick, Certified Spiritual Director,
www.besidepeacefulstreams.com

(*Humming Words*)

Nancy Warwick's poems are beautifully crafted word paintings that reveal forgotten moments in time to be rediscovered, new perspectives to be examined, and glimpses of beauty to be pondered as portraits that go straight to the heart.

—Esther Bryan, Manager & Fibre Artist, The Quilt of Belonging,
Governor General's Award Recipient, Williamstown, Ontario

In *Humming Words: A Collection of Poetry*, Nancy has woven together words into powerful images of life and faith. The poems are inspiring and thought-provoking.

—Rev. Carey Jo Johnston, Managing Director, LEI-Canada

(The Blueprint: Finding Your Spiritual Purpose and Identity)

I enjoyed reading *The Blueprint*; It's purposeful, prophetic, pastoral, personal, practical and a great tool for ministry leaders.

—Rev. Rich Janes, former President Master's College and Seminary, Peterborough, Ontario

In "*The Blueprint: Finding Your Spiritual Purpose and Identity*" Peter Cusick and Nancy (Warwick) Kingdon elaborate on the great truths in Ephesians such as: personal identity in Christ, gifts and calling, leadership that equips the church to be the missional family of God and spiritual authority. With that foundation they do us the great service of applying those truths to not only the individual's life but also the corporate life and structure of a local church. The genius of this book is that it clearly demonstrates how an entire church can experience that their "…sweet spot in life is the intersection of your greatest strength and your greatest passion."

—Rev. David Wells, General Superintendent, The Pentecostal Assemblies of Canada (PAOC)